Chapman

KV-374-655

Voices of the North

*Illustrations by Mary Gibbons,
Alistair Niven and Mike Spring*

Photographs by Marc Marnie

ISBN 0 906772 82 6   ISSN 0308-2695   © *Chapman* 1997

4 Broughton Place, Edinburgh EH1 3RX, Scotland
Tel 0131–557 2207   Fax 0131–556 9565
Editor: Joy Hendry   **Assistant Editor: Samuel Wood**
*Volunteers: Valerie Brotherton,
Christina Cree, Sarah Edwards, Eva Frischläger, Koert Linde, Caroline Lindsay,
Gerry Stewart*

Submissions:

*Chapman welcomes submissions of poetry,
fiction and critical articles provided they are
accompanied by a stamped addressed envelope
or International Reply coupons*

Subscriptions:

	Personal		Institutional	
	1 year	2 years	1 year	2 years
UK	£14	£26	£19	£35
Overseas	£19/$32	£35/$59	£23/$39	£42/$69

THE SCOTTISH **ARTS** COUNCIL

•EDINBVRGH•
THE CITY OF EDINBURGH COUNCIL

Printed by EconoPrint, Salamander Street, Leith, Edinburgh.

Editorial

The death of Sorley MacLean in November last year is a blow to us all. Recently, many of that great generation have gone: Sorley, Norman Mac-Caig, George Mackay Brown, Tom Scott – and just before Sorley, the playwright George Byatt. It is impossible to quantify what they have added to our lives – all of them highly individual, uniquely talented, inspirational.

Sorley's contribution to Gaelic, to Scottish culture generally, is inestimable. His own poetry is exquisite, full of emotional power and honesty, and impelled by an uncompromising intellect. He did so much for the Gaelic language, through his work, personal agitation, and his activities in the field of education: he advanced the status of Gaelic as a poetic language on the world stage, and socially within its own heartland. As a person he was inimitable, a man of incredible magnetism – very much a poet. No-one who heard him read will forget the impact of his voice, underlying and emphasising the impact of his poetry. He was the most valuable of friends, ever generous, concerned with the welfare of those he was in contact with, down to the minutiae of daily life. We will all miss him terribly, and commiserate with his family in their great loss.

Sorley died only days before *Chapman*'s *Tones of Destiny* event at the Assembly Rooms, Edinburgh, intended primarily as a celebration of Scotland's indigenous languages, Scots and Gaelic, but also to honour and celebrate his own achievement. With the family's blessing, the event went ahead, and we were able to use it as a tribute to him. Extracts from the evening were broadcast the following night on Radio Scotland's *The Usual Suspects* and also in late December on *The Radio 2 Arts Programme*. All present, both performers and audience, were acutely conscious of his absence, but intent on making positive and joyous remembrance of this unique man. Sheena Blackhall's poem 'Lament fur the Bard', written specially for the occasion, is published here.

Tones of Destiny was also intended as a fundraiser for *Chapman*'s Lottery bid, which I'm pleased to announce has been successful, the magazine and its publishing having been awarded almost £20,000. Final accounts for the event are not yet available, but from our Lottery appeal to readers and subscribers, approximately £2,000 has already been raised. There is some way to go, but we are confident of reaching our target of £5,000, which will enable us to transform our operations. I'd like to thank all those who have contributed to the appeal so far, and to welcome further donations to bring us up to required level.

It was an enormous sadness to us that our co-organiser of both *Tones of Destiny* and Norman MacCaig's 85th birthday party, Allan Campbell, died in a tragic accident just before New Year. Allan was both a close personal friend, and someone who worked tirelessly to promote *Chapman*, chiefly through his work at the Assembly Rooms.

Finally, I'd like to apologise to Peter McCarey and Owen Gallagher, whose work appeared incomplete due to errors in the typesetting process.

Tones of Destint Photographs

Sheena Blackhall

Lament fur a Bard:
a tribute to Sorley MacLean

The waves o the warld, dunt at the herbor waa
A skirlin skurrie brakks frae the gurly faem
"I cairry bitter news frae the Western Isles
The tides rin wersh, at the daith o the Great MacLean."

A shag gaed slidderin doon the stormy strand
Grave cloots, its wings, as blaik as the gapin mool.
An cauld, its skreich rang oot ower the ocean's mane
"The Lan o the Gael this nicht, is steeped in dool."

"A new birk grows," cry the geese, "in Hallaig's wid.
Its eildritch leaves shine gowd in the dour Deid Thraa
Its sap is the lear o the starns, an the Mapamound
The lear o the auncient Bens, an the robin, sma."

Dowie, the dun deer liftit its heid tae list
The spurgie held its wheesht in the willow tree
"Oh Raasay's beatin hairt's in a timmer kist
He his jyned the shades, in the Glen o Eternity."

"He wis the torc, on Scotia's grizzled craig
The thrum o its clarsach, thrillin abeen the corn
In the mids o war, he'd pause tae murn a foe
Tho lesser men, gied sic puir stock o the scorn."

"MacLean wis a dauncin flame in a drift o snaa
A quaff o hinny ale in a droothy throat
A seannachie, o infinite pouer an grace
He wis the win, in the sail of Gaeldom's boat"

The waves o the warld, sab at the herbour waa
The pulse o the Norlan, freezes in the vein
The keenin wins, rise in the coronach
"The star of the West has set. Sleep weel, MacLean."

True Thomas

Alan MacGillivray

Hood, Corbie, Corbie, Gled and Partners,
Solicitors and Writers to the Signet,
Gilmartin's Close,
EDINBURGH.

Lady MacQueen,
Ferlie Palace,
Fernie Brae,
ELFLAND.

Dear Madam,

Former Employee: Thomas Rhymer.

We have been instructed by our client, Mr Thomas Rhymer, Huntlie Bank, Ercildoune, Border Region, to communicate with you as a matter of urgency anent his recent dismissal after seven years' unbroken employment by you in the capacity of Personal Assistant. Mr Rhymer wishes us to present to you a statement of certain grievances which he feels you have tended to ignore over a long period. We would appreciate it if you could respond positively to the points we shall make and consider the case that they suggest for some kind of compensation to Mr Rhymer in respect of unfair treatment and distress which he claims to have suffered and to be currently still enduring.

The first matter that we wish you to consider is the agreement of employment which Mr Rhymer entered into with you seven years ago. Mr Rhymer tells us that initially he was favourably disposed to accept your offer, which seemed attractive for a number of compelling reasons. He was flattered that you had sought him for the job in question, 'head-hunting' him at his place of residence as a suitable employee. He was given the impression from the elegance and opulence of your dress and means of transport that your business enterprise was in a flourishing financial condition. He further states that he was offered certain inducements of an intimate personal nature to persuade him to accept your offer. We shall return to this point later under another heading. It is our client's contention, and we tend to agree with him, that no valid binding contract of employment was offered to him in written form. Indeed our client has only a vague memory of a verbal agreement in the following terms: "Now ye maun go wi' me, and ye maun serve me seven years, thro' weal or woe as may chance to be." It seems to us that there is a point here to be answered about possible irregularity in your employment of our client, since there appears to be no evidence of normal executive hiring practices being followed, for example, advertisement of post with its conditions and remuneration, preparation of a short leet of suitable candidates, and selection after interview by a properly constituted panel.

The second matter we would raise with you is the question of our client's remuneration in the post. Mr Rhymer represents to us that the offer and acceptance of employment were rushed through without his having any opportunity to negotiate with you on essential matters such as basic salary, transfer of pension rights, National Insurance, bonuses and expense account. We find it difficult to believe, but our client assures us that it is the case, that you never actually made him any monetary payments but paid him in kind with board, lodging, clothing and sundries. Mr Rhymer cites one particular occasion when you presented him with an apple from the garden, saying that this was his wages. The question that we have yet to agree with our client is whether or not this aspect of his employment merits consideration by the Low Pay Unit.

One particular grievance of our client concerns a special bonus or unsolicited gift from you to him along with the aforementioned apple, a gift which you apparently described as "the tongue that can never lie". This falls totally outside our professional field and range of experience so that we find it difficult to envisage what the gift consisted of or what monetary value it represents, but our client insists that it has been merely an encumbrance and a handicap to him all the time it has been in his possession. Mr Rhymer claims that it has blighted his life in a number of ways both during his period of employment by you and since. He has been unable to indulge in any successful and profitable business transactions because of it; his social life and personal relationships have significantly suffered; and, particularly in recent months, he has found it an effective bar to employment in the public services, i.e., for posts sought with Border Regional Council, Roxburgh District Council, and the Lothians and Border Constabulary, as well as jobs in public relations and personnel management with companies like British Steel, and in journalism. We feel that, with good will, there should be the possibility of your taking back this unwanted gift in exchange for a more tangible financial bonus.

We turn now to the conditions of employment which Mr Rhymer was compelled by you to follow. Our client's most notable grievance concerns the unreasonable residence requirement of his job, forbidding him to return to his own home for the period of his 'contract'. As a result of this, his family life and friendships have suffered and the fabric of his dwelling house has deteriorated through lack of maintenance, seriously affecting its market value. Our client further claims that excessive conditions of silence and confidentiality about your business affairs were laid upon him, accompanied by what amounted to illegal threats of retaliation if any confidence was broken. Less serious, but nevertheless distressing to our client's dignity, was your insistence that he should wear a distinctive uniform in the post of Personal Assistant. The uniform supplied was unquestionably of good quality, but Mr Rhymer was unhappy about having to appear on all occasions wearing a green suit of eccentric cut and fashion with green velvet shoes. While he was actually in your employment, this was supportable, but since your dismissal of him he has been obliged, because of his straitened financial circumstances and consequent inability to afford

Recent Principal Winners:

1993
Sally Carr, Long Crendon
Mercedes Clarasó, Lauden
Dean Hawksley, Bristol
Ralph Levinson, London
Dorothy Nimmo, Gloucester
Ronald Tomkins, Altrincham

1994
Tessa Chester, Girton
Richard Griffiths, Ware
Tobias Hill, London
Michael Hulse, Köln, Germany
Kathy Page, London
Marcy Willow, Ripon

1995
David Callard, Cardiff
Richard Griffiths, Ware
George Hobson, Paris
Peter Regent, Newport-on-Tay
Nicola Waldron, Bradford
Kearan Williams, Cottenham

1996
Marion Jordan, Newcastle-under-Lyme
Steve Kane, Portugal
Douglas Lindsay, Senegal
Tony Noon, Mexborough
Edward Richardson, Oxford
Sam Willetts, Oxford

* * * * * * * * * * * *

JUDGES: MARTIN BOOTH and PAUL HYLAND

PUBLICATION
Copies of The Bridport Prize 1996 anthology, published by Redcliffe Press, are available from selected bookshops throughout the country or direct from Bridport Arts Centre, South Street, Bridport, Dorset, DT6 3NR, £7 post paid (overseas £8). The 1997 anthology will be published at the end of October 1997.

Follow-up recognition and successes for previous prizewinners include the reading of Dean Hawksley's story *Humming Delilah* on BBC's Radio 4 in March, 1994, and the inclusion of the poems by John Gurney, Matthew Francis and Rhona Clark in *The Forward Book of Poetry*. Deborah Randall has published at least two collections, Atima Srivasta has written three novels, and Mercedes Clarasó has had a collection of short stories published as well as three novels (two of them since winning a prize at Bridport in 1993) and is expecting a fourth to be published in 1996..

Creeds the Printers, Broadoak, Bridport, Dorset. DT6 5NL

The Bridport
prize

Patron: John Fowles

poetry and short stories
1997
Creative Writing Competition

1st Prize £2,500 ❋ 2nd Prize £1,000 ❋ 3rd Prize £500

plus supplementary prizes

BRIDPORT ARTS CENTRE

new clothes, to continue wearing this uniform. To a sensitive person like our client, the offensive and suggestive comments he has been obliged to put up with in the street and in pubs, and especially in the stand at the recent Hawick Rugby Sevens, have been wounding in the extreme.

It should be clear to you that we are now beginning to touch upon matters of emotional and psychological distress to our client rather than physical or financial damage. There are two other matters that seem relevant to us under this heading and that require to be mentioned before we come to perhaps the most serious grievance uttered by our client. The first of these complaints concerns the fear and alarm caused to Mr Rhymer on his first meeting with you, and on many subsequent occasions, by what he claims was your reckless and aggressive driving while he was your passenger. He quotes you as glorying in the speed of your transport, saying "whene'er her bridle rung, her steed flew swifter than the wind", undoubtedly endangering not only you and our client, but all other road users. A second matter of distress to our client, yet one where the details are unclear to us, has to do with an occasion on a journey when he claims to have been compelled to wade up to his knees in human blood. We would welcome clarification of this point. Does it imply an involvement of our client in a serious motorway accident, perhaps related to his complaint about your driving? There seems to be a need for police liaison here. At the very least, it may highlight a lack of provision by you of suitable protective clothing and footwear.

The final grievance that we would like you to comment on for our client is in our opinion the most serious matter and one that we are contemplating pursuing through the appropriate formal channels. Mr Rhymer is alleging that from the beginning of his employment right through to the time of his dismissal, he was subjected to treatment that, in both his and our opinion, amounts to sexual harassment of a particularly blatant and aggressive kind. Professional caution and good taste prevent us from going into too much detail at this time. However, two episodes described by our client will serve to make the point for the moment. He recalls that, when you offered him the post at your first meeting, you made an overt sexual advance to him, suggesting that if he kissed you on the lips, you would be, in your own words, "sure of his body". Mr Rhymer admits that, in the excitement of the moment, he was imprudently swayed to take advantage of your offer, a course of action which he has since found cause to regret. Our client claims that later, on the journey to your place of business, you turned off the road into a lay-by near a major roundabout and, under the pretext of discussing the correct exit leading to your premises, drew his head down upon your knees and enticed him to further acts of a sexual nature. Without being more specific, we have statements from Mr Rhymer that thereafter, at frequent intervals throughout his period of employment, you forced your unwelcome attentions upon him whenever the fancy took you. We have corroborating statements of a similar nature from another former employee of yours, a Mr Thomas Linn. We regard this as a matter of the utmost gravity and would welcome the opportunity to discuss it with you before we feel compelled to proceed before a tribunal on Mr Rhymer's behalf.

In the light of the foregoing alleged grievances, we feel that there is a strong prima facie case that Mr Rhymer has been wronged in a number of important ways in respect of his former employment by you. We would welcome your cooperation in arriving at a mutually satisfactory conclusion of the matter, which would undoubtedly involve agreed adequate compensation of our client in redress of his grievances. Unfortunately, without such cooperation and compensation, we should feel obliged to make representations to an Industrial Tribunal and also to consider raising an action in the Sheriff Court.

In the expectation of your courteous and prompt attention to this matter, we remain

> Yours faithfully,
> James Corbie
> (for Hood, Corbie, Corbie, Gled and
> Partners, Solicitors.)

Taped Message:

"Elspeth, Bill Hood here. I've just seen the copy of this letter you did for Jimmy Corbie and that he's sending out on behalf of our client, Thomas Rhymer. Jimmy certainly hasn't got any less intimidating in his prose style now he's a full partner. 'Anent' indeed! What I wanted to say was this all sounds very fishy to me. I think we're going to have trouble with this one. Ask Jimmy to have a fly around and find out more about this crazy MacQueen woman. The address seems odd to me. Tell him to get confirmation of it, postal code and telephone number if poss. If necessary he can send his brother Alec to see her. From what Rhymer tells us, she has some big crumbling place out in the wilds. He mentioned hearing the sea on the way there, and going through a kind of desert and also flooded roads, but it was at night so he couldn't really see anything. Sounds as if it might be over in Fife, maybe near Cowdenbeath. I'll ask around at the golf club, bound to be some of the county set who know of her. She sounds like one of the pearls and green wellie brigade who dash around in old Bentleys running traditional Scots fare restaurants, all recipes for howtowdie and bracken wine. Man-mad all of them. Of course, there is the possibility that Rhymer, if that is his name, is just having us on. I've seen it before. Fantasies of sexual slavery and bondage, and it takes us weeks to find out they're all in the mind of some weedy school teacher or frustrated writer from Shotts. If I'd to put money on it, I'd bet that we'll find there isn't a word of truth in anything the chap says."

Corbies

Alan Macgillivray

To the Kingis privy sicht.

drumfreys.

Maist he prince sen i ha ressavit your graceis commissioun to ryde in till annandaill to speir anent the vanissyng of schir iohne irving be it kent that i tuk wi me wat heslop my britheris man squere gilbert douglass the frensch halie fr. jehan de touraine and ducan macdonal the hieland aixman wi fouir lele men mair of my lord maxwellis following. We lugeit weill but thriftilie at muffatt and cam doun by to the castill of lochmabene quhar met us the warden schir andro stewart and his depute iames iohnstone of brydekirk quha undertuik on the mornes morne to leid us quhidder informatioun fra sindry fowk on land had tald o schir io. irving his hors after being spyit lowse rinnyn amiddis thir commounis kail and corn.

Fell air betwix the sun and the sky the mornes morning we rade oot endlang the annan watter binna ane o the lord maxwellis men quha had oouir dronken and wald na fra his bede the quhilk wes a canny childe thon day. Quhill we yeid did schir iames iohnstone mak me acquant wi aa materis anent the vanissyng short syne of your graceis frende and lele man io. irving quhow that he wes to the huntin gane ae day wi hawk hors and mekill doig and niver mair seen by ony man ather gentill or sempill. Quhow that his guidwife the leddy maryane did sair greit and sek easedom fra hir kizzen wm. airmstrong him that scars eschapit hingyn ouir twa murthrys in liddesdail. Quhow that the afoirsaid wm. airmstrong ha sweerit on the haly buik afore the shireff crichtone ar dumfreys that he lay in bede fouir dayis of a fevef in annan and his men did sweer the sam aith.

We cam doun to schir iames iohnstone his castill of bryidkirke short quhill eftir noone and thar did his wyf entretane us weill wi venaison bannockis and guid aill afore we raid fyrthir. The leddy iohnstone commendis hir hartly serviss to yr grace and prayis you to rest in hir hous quhan nixt you ryde to yr border huntin quhidder of the hart or of reivin grahamis.

Nou cumis the hert o my taill anent this matere for quhen we had rid to the length o warmonby towre betwix brydekirke and annan thar cumis rinnan to us sondry hindis and puir cottar fowk beseikin schir iames and his following to kerry aid and soccouris thidder quhar the land ny ecilfechane wes herriet be ane cumpanye of inglis cumberland men be report mair nor xxxv. To the quhilk supplicantis did schir ias. declair his entente to ryd haim to brydekirke for the gaidderan o men and vivaris fra quhens he wald til ecilfechane for the punissyn thir inglis reivaris. Than did i schaw my commissioun and declar myn purpois to gang about yr graceis matere by myn awne wille and rewle. Sa we sindert oor cumpante he gangand ae gait yr servaunt the tithyr.

Quhill that we restit oor hors and powneis fornent wormonby the hielandman macdonal espyit ane mekill fleicht o corbie crawis distrublit and skriechin ouir and amiddis the derk shawis o chapill crois. Than did wat heslop tak hors and gang speidilie thon airt seikin caus o thir briddes distres the lave o wis followin wi wappounis on schaw and redy. Seemit me mair lyk matere o bogill or faerie nor of beastis or mannis weir sen cam na soun of vois nather ding of armoure bot anerly the squakin o thir blak birddis and forby ane unco skreman as of hielan banshy yt stoppit nocht and gert fr. jehan cry his orisounes and ducan macdonal swear gret othes in erse toung. Lykwise did i hald in minde quhow thir reportis erlier avisit anent schir io. irving his hors rinnan wilde did mak mentioun o mekill crawis yt did leid the beaste the airt o the chapellecroce.

Trublit wi thae thochtis i wes war o wat heslop cumin wi mekill hast cryin a murthyr and coccour quhareat we mad gret sped to meet him and quhan he gat neir did heir him speik distract anent blak freiris and spangyairtlyk painis of inquisitioun lyk to a sathane masse or warlock artis. Than did we debait quhat wes best to don ather to gang bak as urgeit my lord maxwellis men or gang forrit as sayd fr. jehan and the aixman macdonal het for the fecht. squere gilbert did mak ane bitter jeste upo the maxwellis quhow that they wald raither a gudewill wauchte or hielan tochantorus than to fecht lyk lele men for theyr lorde or king halie crist quhilk was ane hard sayinge but did nocht gude for that thir cravenis turnit hors and raid for brydekirke as speedie as jockeis on leithe sandis. For quhilk ressoun i pray yr grace to hae wordis wi my lord maxwell touchyng the tressoun of his menyie on yr graceis he affairis leavan bot v. servauntis of yr grace fornent the blakest feendis o hell and of thame the afoirsaid wat heslop nae better nor a yammerin bairn in his fricht.

Takken hert fra the benisounis seyd by the halie fr. and sindry bumman and vauntis by hieland dunkane than did we mak forrit til the skirtis o the chapillcross shawis wi the skrieghis o hellis foulis and demonis bizzin in oor luggis quhar we did stay fute on sicht o glaumry lichtis that schane sklentin atwix the bussis and rochis and hiech treis o the wuid. Eftir schort counsall wi gilbert i gaif command to the aixman anf fr. jehan quha were nocht trew scottis blude and kin that they gang afore us twa quha wald leave daft wat his lane and follow close ahint. Sa we made forrit agayne cumin at lang and last upo the middis o the wuid and a roun open bit o girss the quhilk wes aa brent wi fyr and blak wi ess an aizlis quhar stade a fairie knowe maist lyk but of a schene as it wer siller or the bricht steel of swerdis and a port or gateslap agee in its side thurgh the quhilk wes passand monkis or freis in blak habit wi hudis ouir heidis and grunyies. Sindry freiris cairriet bricht cruzies wi warlockrie lichtis mair nor candell culd gie quhill that itheris cairriet the trew instrumentis and wappounis of sathanis realme the quhilk wald blast me to speke anent. Fra oot the port of the faerie knowe ther cam the frichtsum skremin nois o the quhilk i spam afore.

The warst and veriest deedis of hell lay manifest upo the girss na fer fra quhar we stuid amang the treis and that wes a mekill kist of siller schene in the quhilk ane devillis freir wes stowin lyk banis in a deidkist the corp and airmis and schankis of a naukit manne quhilk as i lukit aghaist did muve and stirre lyk lievan flesch yit wes ther nane bluid or ony guttis. Last

did the servaunt of baal lift hiech a heid that bare the face and semblant
of yr graceis true and pittous sleyn lel man schir io. irving as i have sene
him in the lyf reid and sonsie in the cheke and smilan lippis as it wer at
yr graceis levee or turney at the halyruid or kingis park or gangand be the
cowgait to purchas his milke and kebbuck. i cryit oot lyk man gulliegawit
wi a scherp cuttie and than horrour tae bing on horrour did the heid luik
roun and see me quhar i stude atween the trees than smile lik man at ease
in ony taverne and speer hou wes i this guid even and cryit me by name
as jamy fleming quham last he saw at hugmanie in falkland pallice the
quhilk wes trewe at every pointe. Than did he saye to me not to feare for
that he wesna deid but raither translatit fra oot this mortal corp intil a body
baith eterne and ever younge and that he wes to gang wi his new menyie
of sapient servauntis to a kintra ayont the sternis. At that the freir tuke the
heid stowin it in the kist syne shut the tap an yokit tae cairrie it awa to the
fairie knowe.

Quhill that i stude lyk man indreme than did ducane macdonal and the
fr. jehan rin forrit fra the wude the ane wi mekill lochquhabbir aix heich
abune the heid an cryan a duniewassil slogan the tither haudin up his crois
and halie beadis to cry doun the powris of hevin upo thir demonis and
warlockis. As i lukit in dumfounder did aa the devillis freiris and theire
minionis of corbys and hudies quhilk fleeit as espials and keekeris abuin
i the lift rin and flee and slidder intil the fairie knoe, bot anerly the freir
quhilk barit upo his bak the kist wi io. irvingis fals corp athin. Him did the
macdonal cut in twa piecis wi his michty aix and caus to drap the kist upo
the blaknit girss spillan the limbis and heid and corp aa ouir ither. Thandid
the port of the knowe close fast and suddyn did the haill uprais in
glamourie licht and lowe heich abuin the wuid and flee awa fra sicht in
the gloamin o the day Squere gilbert douglass quha had gane eftir the fr.
jehan to pou him fra the divellis handis wes sair scaddit be the lowe o the
fleean knowe and liggis still amaist at daith and fr. jehan hes vanissyd fran
this warld claught into the devillis hauld and carriet aff the guid kens
quhar.

Quhan aa wes still agayne than did me and dunkane macdonald
gaidder thegither aa the bittis o the fals schir iohne and the black freir the
quhilkis wer of no erdly mydir borne and aa otheir signes and remaynes
inby the middis of the shawis and cause thaim to be brent in a fyr of wude.
Syne did we bar awa gilbert douglass and leid wat heslop lyk a gowk to
the powneis than raid the length o annan thrugh the mirk nicht. Thar did
we pit baith thir puir laddis in the spytaile o the burgh wi the sum of xx
s. for food and herberwe afore the mornes morne quhan we did ryde to
dumfreys and i did speke privilie wi the shireff crichtone. Sinsyne hae we
causit to be conveyit to the halie nunnes at glasgo the leddy maryane wyf
to schir io. irving for safe kepynge against her speking anent hir
housbondis weirdly condicioun and unmanlyk manere in having na
dealing wi hir in bedde or bowere for the quhilk ressoun she becam leman
to hir kizzen wm. airmstrang. Also hae we causit to be brocht to dumfreys
in arrest the afoirsaid wm. Airmstrang and his men and steikit their
mouthis against their proclaimimg of innocencie in the murthyr of schir

io. irving for the quhilk by your commissioun i hae gart thaim be hingyt athout proces of lawe and that richt speedilie. Also hae i causit preyeris to be seyd in the kirke of the greyfreiris for the saule of fr. jehan de touraine be yr servauntis report droont i the solway and his corp niver fand. Also hae i peyit to ducan macdonal the sum of xv 1. that he may be sustenit and cled for the frensch kingis serviss quhidder he has gane sekin new weiris and fechtis. And so hes the matere bene concludit as weill as amy be don.

Yit in my conclusion michty prince dois yr humill servitour beseik you to be war of fals semblant counsellouris quha may be nocht as they appeare true lele scottismen but raither chaungelingis as wes the unhappie and begylit schir iohne irving or warlockis or divellis familiaris in unerdly flesch and bluid or keekeris of inglond or spanye perchaunce sent to wirk you herm and cause tressoun athin the reaulme of scotland to mak it a land wantan king and counsall and the guid lawis of our faitheris and to mak yr grace a man fer fra the hertis of his subiectis and wantan the luve that ocht to be as dong to the grund of your kingdome makkin it riche for the growin o a fre and strang people. And so may yr grace be kept in safetie by the luve of christ and his angellis.

Yr trewe servaunt to command,
iames fleming, knicht.

Pamela Beasant

Out of hand

I am the bone-cracking heat of light
I direct it to you through spread fingers,
through the holes in my hands.
I am stretched under the burden of my concealing shadow,

I hang in the outer space of your mind.
My image, finally, will utterly fail,
it will not bring you a ghost's idea,
it will not wrap you around with this foreboding.

I am neither matter to your senses
nor a figure in any dimension.
I cannot find your probing fingers
they do not break through.

And shall I shape into woman or man ?
What sockets could contain these eyes' wide fire ?
What chariot of mine could creep so slowly
that I would be discerned for a sigh's length ?

I cannot choose this return.
It will not be careful. I cannot help
but scald the ants from my path.
The heat. The light. The winding-sheet.
These things I am.

Haunted

It's been an elastic time since the death;
compressed, then stretched to oblivion.
A lifetime is like that, your life
must have seemed like that to you.

Now forced through ink on the page, you are
used wantonly. A man,
clever, methodical, you liked silly songs,
and died before I knew you started me,

before I realised who was gone.
Sometimes I try to die the death
you faced; but can't rehearse
the long, black thing, or

free you to do it, shadow puppet
dancing in an artificial light.
If I stood courageously, and still,
would you emerge with substance,

colour? Would you take me utterly
or let me go ? I wish

you wanted to test me,
that you were my green Knight, that involved.

I stumble at death's thin coat-tails,
it doesn't turn; for me,
the hollow eyes will not reveal and burn.
My hand closes on nothing, to a fist.

A face darts and lingers
like a trick of the light; sometimes hard,
strong and bright. A glance
crumbles it in a green flash.

Yasha

QueQues filed, naked, children quiet,

Yasha always went to parties,
his eyes danced and his hair curled
in a way the other children loved.
He was touched by magic,
usually won the games.

babies hidden in bundles of clothes,

Yasha stood beside his mother,
stroking the head of his baby brother.
His father was strong.
Finding them.

found, thrown in anyway.

Yasha filed into the room for a shower,
looked at all the places
where the water would spurt out.
His mother held him urgently,
he shook her off impatiently.
The baby found her naked breast
and drank as the gas poured in.

Darkness racing in their minds,

Yasha died in shock,
was bull-dozed into a pit
spread-eagled over an elderly baker
and a boy from his own town.
His mother and his brother were several layers away.
As the earth went in,
it filled cracks between heads and limbs,
neatly covering them all.

death undoing so many.

The Approach

Drawn into time,
gradually, you come.
With weather-beaten wings
with the desire to make honey
you toss and dither.
Hunting us out.

Does the Earth hang
by a thread ? From where you are
only you know,
or may see it in this way,
spinning in a dangerous arc
as you approach.

Closing in,
You move darkness around time's force,
spy the danger suddenly,
prepare your sting.

Iconoclasm

Lenin; massive, face-down,
trundled off to a retirement park
to stand beside himself and Stalins,
(and the KGB man with all the zzzs,)
in a strange, still, parliament of clones.

The people jeer euphorically.
I understand why, but I am sorry
for the smashed up eyes,
the broken dream.

And the mob, though probably right,
are ugly.

Tom's arrival

I broke apart and you came
in the rush and twist, fist first, of your birth;
face folded up against the rasp of air.
And my breast loomed larger than your head.

My midwinter boy.
We lay in our storm abatement.
The rain pounded the roof
while you slept.

Are You Moved ?

David Punter

I can't see you, you know. I can't see you at all.

But that isn't going to stop me telling you my story, I promise you that. There doesn't seem to be anyone else around, does there? I can tell you about her; about the almost liquid snap of her bones – can that be right? Or perhaps it was the light that was liquid – the light has always been very important, you could almost call it a *leitmotif*, ha ha, running through my story like a thread, you might say, yes, that's what it's like.

I didn't use to know words like that; not at the beginning, but I've had time to read, time to think. I always did read a lot, out on the drab streets; I would read walking home from school. I think, looking back on it, that it was the stories where the narrator was right at your elbow I liked best, or over your shoulder, breathing on you, so that you forgot to breathe yourself . . .

You remember the Poe story, the one about the cellars and the sherry? At the beginning there, right next to you, breathing on you: "The thousand injuries of Fortunato", how does it go? "But you, my reader, who know so well the inmost recesses of my soul"; could he have been that smart? Because it's the inmost recess in which he walls him up, isn't it, at the end, in the dark, with nobody to hear his screams, the rattling of the chains.

No, I still can't see you, at all; but did you move just then? I thought I heard something scraping, something in the dark; a claw maybe. I don't know.

But I wasn't exactly what you'd have called a studious youth. Oh no; I knew how to take care of myself. I always was smart; you've probably been noticing, if those are eyes, these creases in my trousers, my perfect colour coordination. I've always liked khaki. A lot of the people in there did, they fancied themselves as hard men, terribly deluded a lot of them were. I remember Paulie; he used to say he'd been three years in the German navy, but the doctors never believed him; at least, I don't think they did. Neither did I. I ask you: would they have taken on a man with a gut like a whale and a habit to match? Anyway, he didn't seem so tough after I did those things to him . . .

But never mind. Are you making yourself comfortable in there?

Did I put you there? I can't remember now. But I do remember the light starting. I was twelve, I think it was (unless, of course, at that time I was another person altogether – but we'd prefer not to canvass that possibility, wouldn't we? It could be so unsettling). I wasn't reading then, I was walking, through the suburbs, under the ornamental cherries, I think they were, a hot day, I thought to start with it was the parked cars, something about the sunlight bouncing off them, but then it seemed to take over; I was looking into a mass of light, oh it was ... what was it?

Sit still, I'm trying to think. It was like all the light in the world, bunched up and swirling; I couldn't see anything through it, not the street, not the cars, I didn't know which way up I was. It was like a greeting. It was as though maybe there was somebody behind the light, somebody trying to make contact, but I didn't care. I just sort of settled down inside myself. I was conscious of being hard, hard all over, and sitting crouched inside myself, looking out at this world of light. Very watchful, I was, because you never knew; you never knew who or what might come through it . . .

And then it started to happen quite often. I never could make it do it, though. But then, you can't, can you? I know that because I've seen my notes: "delusions developing into enveloping hallucinatory states" – they thought at first it was something to do with my eyes. I suppose it was, in a way. Ah – you may have noticed that I'm talking in the past tense. Very astute of you. Well, it's true: they're gone now. That's how I come to be here, I suppose. What do you think? Do you think they let me out? Ah well. Maybe they did, maybe not. You don't know yet, do you? That's because I haven't finished my story, tra-la; not time for beddy-byes yet. Do you remember, I wonder, being read to by your mother (or by my mother, come to that – it's always possible, you know). Do you remember that moment when the story sort of takes off, when you know, maybe it's only for a split second (have you ever split the second?), that you're falling asleep, you're losing control, all the sharp outlines and creases in the world, all the neatnesses of the story, all of that is bunching down into a soundless explosion, and after that it'll only be dreams, hiatuses, gaps, that other world which is silent light . . .

I don't know whether you would know that or not. I'm not at all sure what manner of thing I've got here, or how you came to be there. Did I put you there, I wonder? If I did, why would I have put you where I can't see you? Or is it that you have come to me, scrabbling up the sheer sides of a blackness from somewhere ...

Now. The thing is this. I'm trying to tell you about the light, and that's because I'm trying to tell you the real story. Let me try to make it simple. The light, it was like punctuation in my life. Do you understand that? It came at certain points; it seemed to carry meaning, although I never had the slightest idea *what* it meant. Yes, Beckett, he was another one. Watt, and all the rest of them locked away in their rooms, performing mean-ingless repetitions. I've gone in for a bit of that, but it's only really cam-ouflage, it confuses them. Well, you've got to give them something to talk about at their case meetings. I can imagine it now. Here'll be the day nurse, and she'll be saying, "Do you know, he washed his hands fifty-eight times today?" And then the night nurse, he'll say – they were a tough bunch, those night nurses, I'll say that for them – he'll say, "That's a bit strange, Fiona, because at night he spends most of his time shitting on the carpet and smearing it on the walls". And then the psychiatrist will stroke his beard and say, "Hmm, yes, anal compulsive", and then the night nurse will say, all surprised, "Hey, that's right, that's what he smeared on the walls, 'anal compulsive', I couldn't read it at first", and then that gets them all guessing. One night I smeared "Self-consistent narration is a load of baloney" on the walls, well, no I didn't really, there wasn't enough shit, I'm only human, despite what they say, so I only got as far as "self-consist", but even that made them sit up and take notice. But never mind, they found a way to explain it, they tried to get me to say I was receiving messages from some other place, internal broadcasting they call it, so I cooked up these little demons from Mars for them, ha ha, and asked them if they thought I thought my shit was like Mars bars, they didn't like that at all. Mind you, I wouldn't like their job either, especially not with me around.

Anyway, the point is that the light really *is* the story. That's what used to piss me off. They wouldn't believe it, they wouldn't *concentrate*; they kept wanting me to talk about that bloody woman. And, after all, what was there to say about her. Well, a few facts, I suppose. We were married. For a long time. I wonder whether you know her name? You might do, if you can read. It's been in the papers. But can you read? Can you hear? Have you got organs at all, in there, scrabbling, in the dark? Or is it that you used to have them, but now I've gone and done it, I've done those things to you like I did to Paulie and now you don't know where they are anymore, in all that shapelessness, and maybe blood too; I don't know if there's blood. I can't see any seeping out, like it did with Paulie.

You see, the odd thing is that that was far worse, in a way; but then, it didn't count, because I was in there, and so it wasn't my fault, they shouldn't have left me so long with him, well, it was only a couple of minutes, but it was still too long. Obviously, the way things turned out. There was another chap I met in there, what was his name? Ross? Rustin? Ruskin? Dunno. Anyway, he came from one of these families, they didn't have them where I lived, because of course I was respectable (so was she, of course – very respectable) and there was some kind of feud. Tony, that was it, Tony Ross. Maybe. Or something like that. Anyway, this other lot, they'd come to get him. I can imagine it now. The bottles, the slash of glass in the dark, the thud of bodies, the cries of outrage. He was left brain-damaged, but that's when they really started. When he was let out for the first time they came for him again, and burnt half the house down. And it went on from there. Poor chap. I never could stand that kind of thing myself.

But then, I was lucky; because of the light. It gave me something to look forward to, something I knew was coming, something that would always be with me. I was wrong, wasn't I. Well, never mind, it's after the end now, isn't it, in some ways; probably for you, anyway, but then I still can't see what's left of you. Or are you growing in there somewhere?

Hell, maybe I've got this whole thing wrong. Maybe I didn't put you in there, wherever that is. Maybe you've always been in there, growing and stinking; and maybe I'm the one that's pinned here, watching with fascinated eyes while you . . . evolve? deliquesce? are we back with liquid snapping of bones again? I can certainly hear a kind of slither, but there's nothing much new in that.

So what they wanted me to tell was simple: it was the story of her death, of why I'd killed Katie. I did try, at least to begin with, but I couldn't seem to make them see. No vision. I couldn't make them see that it was all too obvious really. I did it because she was in the way. I'd taken every precaution. You see, I realised quite early on that the light didn't come on its own. It was a kind of intensifier, does that make sense? To make light you need light. I imagine God might have said that. Do you have a Maker, I wonder? I wonder . . . this could be one of those hall of mirrors things, couldn't it? When you come out of there (if you do – indeed if you *can*, maybe you're attached, I picture little shiny red threads holding you to the boulder – if there is a boulder. Maybe I'm thinking of some myth or other, doesn't one of the heroes come swooping down and rescue a sea-nymph from a dragon? My schooling, as I've been trying to explain, was decidedly patchy. Because of the light) – when you come out of there, maybe you'll look just like me. But it won't matter; because I won't know.

So what I did was, I didn't used to go out in the streets on sunny days – unless I wanted to, that is. And in the house I'd have the blinds drawn when I wanted, and I'd open them when I wanted. What I didn't like was being surprised by it. Katie understood that; at least I thought she did.

My word, she had a lot to put up with, that woman. Did I say that breezily enough? You've no idea. Well, I couldn't work, of course; it would have conflicted with the punctuation. She did, though, she was a secretary of some sort, I never did know much about what she did. There weren't any mirrors in the house, they might have surprised me. Ah – that's it, isn't it? "Through a glass darkly". I never could quite work out what that meant, any more than Paul, was it, saying it was better to marry than to burn. Burning with desire, was that it, was that what it was about, oh yes, I've had my moments, but through a burning-glass, do you think? I could never get it *out* really, oh, I'd be hard all right, I told you I was a hard man (do you have a carapace, or are you just getting used to me?) but then it all seemed to trickle off down the wrong tube or something. It was the same with writing, for quite a while I thought that might be good, what with all the reading and the light and I thought maybe it was that vision thing but never a single word would come out, they jostled and banged around in my head for a long while, hard words, oh, rock-hard, solid as rocks you rescue dragons from – are you a dragon in need of rescue? Or have I got that wrong again?

So she'd opened the curtains by mistake. It makes you wonder, doesn't it? Twenty-six years married, or eight, or eleven, or some such number, and after all that she goes and opens the curtains when I didn't want them opened. So then it was time for the sound of liquid bones, because I could see the light gathering, bunching, but she was in the way. And what was weird was that she stayed there too, stayed while I 'advanced on her', as they say. Why did she do that, do you think? Why did she open the curtains at all?

Don't worry, those are called rhetorical questions. They're called that because I'm going to answer them myself. Which is ridiculous really, isn't it? I mean, how do you know, how do I know, that I'm going to answer them? Indeed, am I? Who knows? If I don't, would that mean that a rhetorical question suddenly became a non-rhetorical question? Retrospectively, as it were? Is that possible? Can we have retrospective changes in performative status, that's what I want to know. I think we should be told. It's all a conspiracy, that's what it is, ha ha, they loved it when I told them that, conspiracy good God, I used to shout at them eventually, trembling suitably the while, with governments like ours who needs conspiracies?

So I strangled her and threw her down the stairs. I did wonder for a few seconds whether that would help in some way. For example, maybe the light would be even more intense; or alternatively I might get to hear some kind of cosmic giggling. I should have liked to hear that, it would have confirmed something for me.

Oh very good – is that you or me? It's certainly the closest to cosmic giggling – or is it gurgling? – that I've heard yet. Though how to judge approximations to the ineffable, even in its comedic aspect ... Tough one, hey? But don't hesitate to pick up on the jokes if you want to, after all you're the only audience I've got. Or maybe you're the only audience you've got – how do you feel about that? Is that a glint on a carapace? Or do you prefer shell? Or BP? Or Q8 – I've always liked that sign as evidence of the semiotic materiality of the word – it comes from Kuwait, you know, you have always known that, haven't you? But then, I'm being inconsiderate again, I'm assigning senses to you which you may not possess; or, if you ever did possess them, they may now be a dim crimson memory to you through a blood-filled haze. Oh dear, I do hope you're alright in there. There doesn't seem much room; but then who can tell what further caverns you inhabit, to what you might be attached in terms of inner recesses?

I have it. You're an ear. Ah ha. All solved – recesses, red filaments, agonic transformations. Or – ho ho – this is getting better – maybe you're the mortal coil, shuffling off somewhere, not to be born, I'll be bound - 'bourn', 'bound', do you get that? No, you can't, you've certainly got nothing to read with, and some jokes only make sense on the page, and there ain't no paper here, that's for sure, not even to wipe your bum with.

Loose talk costs lives. What I think is – and I shall say this as portentously as I can under these curiously pressing circumstances – is that She Knew Her Time Had Come. That was why she drew the curtains (or were they blinds?) against my express wishes. And that was why she didn't move when I went to move her. Or was that some kind of fascination, mesmerism; or again, is it ever possible to move ... That's the thing, you see, I know how the light looked to me; but how did I look to the light? Was it watching me? or something behind it? Are you watching me? If you are, you'd better be very careful. I don't know whether I can move at all, not after all that, but it's possible, now isn't it? And I might come in there after you, come and clutch your elbow, as it were, or peer over your shoulder, if you've got one. That old bird on the ship might have been in the habit of stoppething one of three, but right here I've only got you. And you got me, babe.

Well, so then there must have been a dreadful clatter when she landed amid the brooms and hoovers and whatever other household detritus no doubt occupied our lower landing, although I can't remember ever relating to any such things, because by the time the light had faded and I was returning grimly but with my usual gritty determination to the half-shades and different beauties of a dusky evening they were pouring all over me (or do I mean pawing?) – lots of uniforms, white coats, all that sort of thing. It's corny, that bit. I mean, what would have been better would have been if they'd swooped in from above like – was it Perseus? yes it was, wasn't it, what a triumph of memory over extreme adversity – and better still, it was Andromeda, yes it was, but what was the name of the poor bloody dragon? No, there you have me, as they say, and as no doubt the dragon did too before it went off to do its bit of cosmic gurgling. Or would it have been comic gargling? I suppose it would depend on how it saw itself . . .

And that brings me to another point, which might well be my last, or failing that yours. Which is this seeing yourself business. The unexamined life isn't worth living, right? Socrates said that. Well, so did I. I used to be obsessed with that (I use obsession strictly in the lay sense, otherwise you might think I'm a bit touched). With trying to see myself, when I knew I couldn't, because if I did the whole dark background might come crashing in. Or failing that (I'm beginning to like that phrase) I might be absorbed forever into planes of light. That might seem fun to you, mate, but that light was also like a bunched fist, that's what it was like, I was occasionally taken aback by the extremity of its potential for violence. It all takes a bit of getting used to.

Well, are you getting used to it? Being in there, I mean? Did you enjoy my story? I hope you're not making a mess in there, shedding bits of skin, exuding entrails, that kind of thing, because somebody's got to clear up after you, haven't they? Are you coming closer, or is it me? Here's a good closing line, a line on which we might close with each other: Is it getting darker, or is it just my imagination? I can hear the scrabbling, though, and maybe those are points of light, are they eyes? Can you see me as well as hear? Are you – tell me, seriously – are you moved?

George Gunn

The Sky Walkers

A woman walked to the sky
she whispered my name
I turned into a baby
& lay at her feet in a cradle of dunes

& who put us there
the persistant storm
the usual harvest
or the tides & the salmon?

No. We were there
by tractor
& combine
& the bigger hell of everything

Plastic Daffodils

Once you came here from a sale
with a bunch of plastic daffodils
as June impersonated Summer
the sledge of the surf echoing on the beach
you a one man Mardi Gras,
a mock chief with a clowns rattle
just like the circus of the weather
& because the real flowers had died
to spread the little joke a hillfire
further while you argued with your wife
I planted them in Wordsworthian clumps
along the borders & beneath the trees
yellow too yellow & green too green
where lupins & pansies sat & pouted
"My, wid ye look on those blooms"
gasped an amazed Annie Calder
"How did ye get them lek thon
so late on?"
"Uh!" my mother replied
the stolen pride of an ego's failing
leaving the words hanging on the line
where her pegs should've been
"It's all in the watering."
"My, but is it no choost great
what they can do nowadays?"
So now, despite history

Mike Spring Illustration

& that parabolic yellow curving smile
& the flowers that will not grow
to be suspended thus in the garden
that grew nothing but stones & rhubarb
that caught every wind like it was an old friend
in there you captured
two pounds fifty & a lucky bag
a cattle thief's boy & a blacksmith's son
& all our systems gone wrong
I still see you
the gaunt hope of favour
hanging like smoke
from those plastic daffodils
& little did I know
that they would change my mind
& catapult me into dressing rooms
arguing with directors & producers
who knew far more than me
but none had glimpsed
the gin soaked Kenya
the Kay's catalogue
the sweat oozed hell
of those plastic flowers
to see them once & pass on
a Caithnessian impossibility
we suffer, then we live

Miracle

Ernest Saunders was sent to jail
for frauding millions from Guinness
No lamentation or rejoicing

issued from any Celtic heart
as he took up his residency
Poor Ernest developed Alzheimer's Disease

& the lack of cash was so intense
they let him out & strange
to say he regained his cash

& miracle! he being, to date
the only one from the Disease
of Alzheimer to make a full recovery

The Scots leid an ither wee toungs: hou kin Scots haud up in Europe?

Nigel Grant

We kin finn in the warld the day a fouth o ensamples o a whien o leids, wan o whilk hes aye ettled tae be the anerlie leid o its kinn. This is commoun aa ower Europe, in a time o chynge; time chynges the picture. Some leids hae deed, ithers kud be on the pynt o daith, an yin or twa maybe hae kam tae life agin. We see it in Spain, whaur Spanish (Castilian), Galician (whilk is gey neir tae Portuguese), an Catalan forebye, (whilk is hauf-wey atween Spanish an French), kin nou aa coexiest. This wesnae aye sae. In the time o Franco, anerlie Castilian had onie place avaa, an Catalan (an Galician, an Basque) wesnae permittit in the press or in the schuile, aiven on the telephone or in publick. A frien o mine yit minds, in his bairntime, speikin Catalan wi his faither on the bus, bein tellt bi a polis, *"¡Hey! ¡Hable cristiano!"* (Speik Christian!) Catalan, the ornar leid, hed nae place avaa, an the schuiles ettled tae turn the bairns oot aa as Spaniards, an naethin else.

This chynged, aiven afore Francos daith, when his regime gan tae be forfochten, an chynged completelie wi the restaur o democracie tae Spain. Nou, thai kin hae baith Spanish an Catalan in Catalonia, wi Catalan oot in front. Thai arna aa that close, but fur a Spanish speikar tae leir Catalan or Potuguese (gin thai ettle) isnae unco haurd, an fur a Catalan or a Gallego tae leir Spanish is fur ordnar. Sae in Spain, giean the wull, leistweys in the tradietional autonomous provinces, the grun is stellt fur effective bilingualism.

In Scandinavia, the leids ar sae neir at leirin the ithers isnae necessair avaa. Gey few Danes leir Norwayan, or the ither wey roon. Yin or twa dae, bot the leids ar sae close at no monie finn this needfu. Thai ar diefferent, bot like eneuch tae yaise yer ain in converse wi the ither. This isnae anerlie in converse, bot on mair formal occasiouns tae. Fur ensample, ma frien Thyge Winther-Jensen, o the Univairsitie o Copenhagen, tuk his Doctorat a few yeir syne at the Univairsitie o Oslo. Nou, he screivit an presentit his thesis in Danish. Then cam the examination, whilk is a muckle event in Scandinavia. It lastit twa days: twa lectures, yin on a subject thai wale, an anither on a theme walit bi the candidat. Thair wes twa extern examiners, as we caa thaim; thai caa thaim 'opponents'. Yin wes a Norwayan, an the ither a German wha, byornarlie, speiks guid Norwayan (whilk is gey unco).

Maist o the time, Thyge wes speirit at in Norwayan, an andswered in Danish, wes speirit at in Norwayan, an sae forrit. On the saicant day, he gied his lectures in Danish, wes speirit at in Norwayan gied, repone in Danish. Thair wes nae problem. At the enn, he wes tellt at he hed passit, an the doctorat wes bestowed on him. Nane o this gied oniewan onie fyke avaa.

Norwayans, Danskers an Swades yaise thair ain leids wi wan anither. Nou, thir leids ar aa gey lik wan anither, bot thai ar no identical. Thair ar twa kinns o Norwayan; Riksmål (govern speik, spak bi maist o the fowk) luiks lik Danish, on the page; bot the soon kythes orra, aiven mair orra than Inglish spak bi a Scot kin soon tae an Inglishman. The ither is Nynorsk, New Norwayan, whilk wes stellt oot o Landsmål (kintra speik) efter self-staunin. Baith hae equal status, in the schuile, in the coorts an in pairliament. Swadish is a wee bit mair diefferent in vocabular an grammar, an maist o aa in soon. Sae Danskers an Swades hae tae cock thair lugs an tak mair tent tae yin anither, bot thai kin aa dae it. It's a lang time syne Denmark hed pouer ower Norway, an neir as lang syne it wes thocht at Norwayan wes 'bad Danish'. Fur aa Scandinavians, aa thair leids kin be fremmit, bot thai kin aa be unnerstuid tae.

Aiven mair sae, thai kin aa eithlie reid ilka ithers leids; thai dinna hae tae be owerset. Aiblins thai ar, bot at kin be tae mak a pynt. Fur ensample, anither Danish frien o mine, Knud Wagner, yaised tae edit a journal on educatioun cryit *Pædagogik,* wi monie articles bi monie screivers frae Denmark, Norway, Swaden, America, Germany an Britain. Thai aa sent in thair copie in thair ain toungs, bot Knud had thaim owerset intae Danish. Nou, aabodie in Denmark kin eithlie reid aa the Scandinavian leids, an Inglish, an monie ken German tae. It wesnae fur eith o communicatioun at thai wer owerset, bot fur tae mak the pynt at leistweys wan journal on educatioun kud be publishit aa in Danish. In a kintra wi five meillion fowk (jist lik Scotland), the pynt kythed weill warth makkin. The Scandinavians ar weill yaised tae the idea at the various forms o Nordic exeist. Thai leir aboot thaim in schuile, an leir tae listen (an tak tent, gin needfu), an kin haunle the diefferences; bot thai kin aa hain an kin speik thair ain, whitiver it is. Thai ken at thai ar aa Scandinavians, bot dinna expeck aabody tae speik the samin. Whaur thair ar diefferences, thai leis thaim an ettle tae unnerstaun. Maist o the time, thai dae, an thai kin haunle ither leids tae. Thai hae leirit, lang syne, at leirin anither leid disnae mean at yer ain hes tae be tint.

Nou, it is weill kent at the Scandinavians ar skilled linguists, bot this skill hes naethin tae dae wi thair genes; that wald be a daft notioun. It hesnae muckle tae dae wi their schuilin either; leids ar takken gey serious, bot thair leirin isnae magick. I hae seen ower monie dreich lessons in a fouth o schuiles tae tak haud o the idea at thai hae developit a panacea.

Naw, the andswar maun be mair ordnar. Thir ar kintras wi muckle lannmasses (Norway an Swaden leistweys) an no monie fowk - aboot fower meillion in Norway, five meillion in Denmark, an aboot nine meillion in Swaden. Thai maun aa communicate wi ilk ither, an in the context o the muckle warld, sae thai aa leir Inglish alsweill as thair ain leids, an maybe German an ither toungs tae. Thai ar internationalists, bot aa kin haud on tae thair ain identite, an kin dae this athoot bummin or vaingloir. Sae, thai ar abell tae haunle thair ain identitie in an international warld. Thair schuiles dae weill eneuch, bot the maist crucial thing is at thair leids dinna dwine awaa, athoot implyin at this maks at oniewan hes tae be heid-bummer either.

The mair we luik aboot Europe, the mair we kin see this kinn o thing. Lang syne, Denmark hauded swey ower Swaden an Norway tae, but this wes anerlie a dynastic union; the Union o Kalmar didnae claim Danish suzeraintie, or hae onie, ower the intern affairs o Sweden an Norway. Swaden brak awaa, an muckle leiter Norway, an aa ar nou self-staunin. This disnae stop thaim the nou frae rinnin an airline thegither, or haein travel atween the kintras athoot passports. Thair bygones hed as muckle fechtin as atween Scotland an Ingland, bot thai ar lang past that stage, an kin tak haud o ilk ithers identitie, an hain thair ain tae.

In the wan-time Soviet Union, the process is at a muckle eirlier stage. The fourtie meillion Russians ootside Russia in the successor states still hae tae sort oot thair relatiouns (an muckle else). We finn, fur ensample, at Ukrainian an Byelorussian nou hae offiecial status, bot this isnae new; aiven afore self-staunin, thir leids wer yaised in publick places an in the schuiles. Russian, tae whilk thai ar gey neir, wes an is commounlie yaised in the touns an in sophisticated culture, in Kiev an Minsk in especial. Russian hed muckle prestige, an monie Russians hed settled thair. Aiven afore self-staunin, Byelorussian an Ukrainian kud be yaised in schuile an fur ither publick purpoises. Self-staunin o coorse hes stellt up in a stranger positioun fur the ither leids, bot monie wull still leir Russian alsweill. In wantime Czechoslovakia, Czech and Slovak ar yaised fur aa purpoises, bot this wes fur ordnar afore self-staunin tae. Czech and Slovak hes a heich degree o mutual intelligibilitie, lik Danish and Norweyan (o baith kinns).

Mair interestin maybe is the sietuatioun in Spain. Catalonia, Galicia, Euskadi (the Basque Kintra) an the Balearic Ilands (whilk speik Catalan as weill) arena totallie self-staunin; thir provinces ar still pairt o Spain, bot hae autonomous status, wi thair ain governs, an control ower schuilin an language policie. Basque is unner pressure wi its muckle populatioun o Castilians, an wi Basque bein a totallie diefferent leid, an haurd tae leir. (The Basque kintra in Spain is a bit mair prosperous, lik Catalonia, an draas fowk in frae ither pairts o Spain fur wark). As is weill kent, aa leids bot Castilian wer banned unner Franco, bot wi the restaur o democracie thir provinces hae kythed autonomous agin.

This chynge is maist obvious in Catalonia. In Franco's time, it wisnae permittit in the schuile, in the kirk, in the press, in publick an aiven on the phone. The nou, it is the normal leid fur aathing. Aiven the Keing (wha speiks Catalan alsweill as Castilian, an is cryit Joan Carles thair, no Juan Carlos) weillcomed the fowk tae the 1993 Olympics wi *"Benvinguts a Barcelona"* (Weillcome tae Barcelona), an Catalan wes spak mair nor Castilian in the opening ceremonie. I hae mairkit at whan I gie a lecture in Barcelona, thai gar me dae it in Spanish, bot I feel an obligatioun tae apologise aforehaun in Catalan. The leid didnae dee whan Franco banned it; it is gey an vieve, an neir aabodie kin haunle Castilian alsweill; monie kin speik French tae, an mair an mair leir Inglish alsweill. Catalonia is confident; its natural identitie needna be incompatible wi bein pairt o Spain, an pairt o Europe tae.

Sae whit's wrang wi the Scots? It's no as we hedna a national leid; we hae twa, the Gaelic an the Scots. We hae the Inglish alsweill; aa o us ken it, the maist speikin it diefferent frae the Inglish. Bot maist o us yaise anerlie the Inglish fur screivin or fur formal speikin leistweys. This is gey orra.

The Gaelic is diefferent, an raxes back tae a historic an lieterarie past. A whein bairns ar tocht in it, bot nae eneuch. It is jist hingin on, an mair maun leir it gin it is to be shair o survival. Sae we hae it, in Glesca alsweill as in Stornoway an Portree, bot maist fowk (leistweys in the Lallans) canna speik or unnerstaun it. Gin we ettle tae get back oor ain leids, we hae twa, an maun wark on thaim baith - no jist the wan, bot the baith.

Efter aa, the day is duine whan we kud think o Gaelic as jist fur the Heilans an Scots as jist fur the Lallans. Sae monie fowk hes movit aboot in Scotland at thair ar mair Gaels in Strathclyde nor in the Eilanan nan Iar, Gaelic in the Lallans an Scots in the Heilans; an thir leids ar *baith* leids o Scotland, an kin haud on tae life an wauk up anerlie here an *naewhaur else*. We hae muckle adventitious leids in Scotland (alsweill as Inglish): Italian, Punjabi, Polish, Urdu, Chinese an a fouth o ithers. Nou, gin Italian or Punjabi deed oot in Scotland, Scotland wad be the puirer fur the loss, bot thae leids wad still be vieve in Italy an the Punjab. Gin Gaelic or Scots deed oot in Scotland, thai hae naewhaur else tae gang; thai wad jist dee.

Bot wi Scots, thair is an unco thing. Sae faur, it hesna deed, bot hes been gralloched. It hes an auncient tradietioun, raxin back mair nor sax hunner yeir in lieterature an leirin. Maist o us kin unnerstaun it in som meisure, an faur monie it is the mither toung, the leid o haem an life an wark. Sae whit is the maitter wi it? Its problem is at it is ower neir tae Inglish, an hes lang been confusit wi a 'dialeck'; aiven Burns publisheit his poems (screivin pairtlie in Inglish) 'mostly in the Scottish dialect', an it hes hed nae ruim avaa in the schuile.

Aiblins, it kin finn a wey intae lessouns fur lieterature - Burns, whiels, or maybe a Border ballant or twa. It maybe kin be recognised fur that, bot it canna eithlie be yaised as a medium. Thair is a whein o schuiles whilk hae duine muckle mair aboot Scots than thai did wance, an yin or twa heidies trate this wi approval. Bot thair is nae glimmer o acceptance in the general life o the schuile. Tae speik the wey bairns yaisuallie speik hes been pitten doon, condemnit as 'bad English', 'coarse speech', 'debased dialect', 'corrupt jargon', an sae on; it is aiven pit oot at Scots is anerlie a corrumpit form o Inglish.

O coorse, historicallie, it is nae mair bad Inglish than Norwayan is bad Danish or Catalan bad Spanish; as far the ither wards o condemnatioun, thai micht staun as a summarie o social jeidgements, but thai ar liguisticallie athoot meinin. The condemnatioun o som kinns o Scots (Glesca fur ensample) fixes intil the glottal stop, as gin wes self-aividentlie coorse or corrumpit; bot thai shud mind at the glottal stop is normal - aiven elegant - in Hawaiian, Arabic an Danish. It's jist a consonant at disnae kythe in Inglish, or leistweys in the 'standard' Inglish.

The tribble wi thir kinn o girns is at thai stell up anither budies set o prejudieces at anerlie Inglish (leistweys, as definit bi the norms o the heichclass Sooth-Eist) is correck, the ither forms tae be dingit doon. Aa ower the warld, thair ar ither wheins o leids, wan o whilk hes grawed tae a posietioun o muckle power an prestige, lik Spanish, French, German Russian, Italian, Putonghua (Mandarin Chinese), Arabic an a fouth o ithers.

Inglish is wan o thae, wan o a whein o North Germanick dialecks at wes brocht intae thae ilands efter the faa o the Roman Empire. Wan o thae gied rise tae Scots, an anither wan tae Inglish. Inglish hes grawed intae muckle commercial an poleitical influence, maistlie frae bein the leid o America, no fur onie intrinsick raisoun, an this posietioun o Inglish in the modern warld itsel maks a guid case fur haein it tocht in oor schuiles. Bot tae gainsay at Scots is thairfur noa leid avaa is tae tirl the logic ower faur.

Thair is nae reason whit wey a bairn canna leir Inglish an hain Scots tae, an leir ither toungs alsweill. We hae ower lang been thirlit tae the notioun o the 'bilingual deficit', the idea at the mense wes a pynt-pot, wi ruim fur anerlie wan leid in yer heid. Leirin Gaelic or Scots or onithin else, bi this notioun, widnae lave eneuch ruim fur Inglish, an thoosands o bairns hev hed thair Scots or Gaelic tocht oot o thaim (or lik wi ma faither, beltit oot); an this hes befaaen hunners o thoosands o ither weans wi ither leids - like Catalan, Basque, Breton, Occitan – at micht 'haud back' thair French or Spanish. This gangs agin ordnar observatioun alsweill as commoun sense. It gangs agin linguistic kennin tae; research in linguistics hes demolishit the 'bilingual deficit' syne the 1960s, an afore that meillions o fowk aa ower the warld hae provit at bilingualism is the internatiounal norm, no the exceptioun.

Bot this attitude an the practices at cam wi it hes shoved Scots tae the mairgins o yuiss. Aiven whan it is yaised, it is wardit tae a gey limited range. Thair is muckle guid poetrie in Scots, aiven a whein gret poetrie, an plantie o drama, feictioun an ither screivin; nanetheless it is baurlie yaised avaa fur expositorie prose. This is a gey damagin lack, makkin Scots available fur anerlie heich screivin or coamick yuiss, bot no fur oniethin serious at is no poetick.

The normal medium fur screivin is prose, sae onie leid at disnae yaise it fur that has tint a register, is gralloched frae the stert, is stuntit. It is crippled in speik alsweill. Maist lik (fur thair arena onie offiecial statisticks) maist Scots kin unnerstaun it tae som extent, an monie kin an dae speik it, maybe fur converse. It kin aiven be yaised in publick fur tellin a joke. Bot it is never yaised fur oniethin tae be takken serious. Fur teachin at schuile or univairsitie, fur polietical speik or airgument, fur flytin, we aa speik Inglish. We kin yaise the orra Scots ward or phrase tae gie it smeddum or saut the discoorse, bot that is jist aboot aa. Scots isnae spak in onie situatioun whaur the content is mair important nor the medium.

This is sae at variance wi the status o a minoritie leid - comparit wi Slovak or Catalan an monie ithers – in screivin an speikin. It maun be a hingower frae the Union o 1707 an later in the eichteinth century, whaun anerlie 'standard English' wes gied onie place avaa in the schuile an in the press. We kin see the effecks o yon in the spellin o the smaa bittocks o Scots at get publisheit. Aiven Burns an MacDiarmid med muckle yuiss o the apostrophe - wa', lo'e, ca', han' fur waa, loe, caa, haun. Nou, the apostrophe is a sign at thair is a letter missin – an sae thair is, bot in Inglish, no in Scots.

Aiven in this, the Scots leid is mairginalised, pitten doon as an orra fremmit (fremmit?) form o Inglish, no in onie wey as a leid in its ain richt. An as lang as the schuiles pey a wee bit o attentioun tae Scots fur lieterature, an maybe fur creative screivin, but rule it out fur aathing else, an no yaise it fur leirin, we ar contriebutin tae the daith o wan o oor native leids.

We need tae wark oot a spellin no basit on the Inglish, an we need tae yaise it, in the mou an bi the pen, no jist fur poetrie an comedie bot fur airgumentatioun tae. We wull finn at monie passages wull no be sae diefferent frae the Inglish, bot that is because a muckle pairt o the vocabular is frae Latin, French, Greek, Norse, Italian an a fouth o ithers, an Scots hes takken frae aa thir leids syne the Middle Ages. The muckle smeddum o Aulder Scots wes its abilitie tae tak wards frae aa leids an mak thaim its ain.

Scots is no ma main leid. I am a Heilander, an wes brocht up in the Heilans; in ma bairntime, the leids wes Inglish an Gaelic. Bot I hae leirit it tae som meisure, fur in ma backgroon, aiven in the Heilans, wes Burns an the Border Ballants - an Oor Wullie an the Broons. I hae leirit monie leids syne, bot thair is a problem wi Scots.

Maist ither leids hae a recognised form, wi the spakken versiouns bein the approximatioun whilk speikers ettle tae keep tae. Maist ither leids ar yaised fur normal airgumentative prose. Bot Scots hes nae standard, and nae prose fur airgument. We ar aa tocht tae dae that in Inglish, Atweill, I ken Inglish aareadie, an hae publisheit muckle in that, an a wee bit in Gaelic alsweill, an ither European leids tae. Bot Scots hes a partiecular problem; thair is nae *standard,* sae maist o the time I hae tae guess at it, or invent it as I gang alang. Ye see the ootcum.

An thair is nae expositorie prose, nae airgumentatioun in Scots. This hes been no ettled syne the seventeinth centurie, as faur as I ken. I am concernit at the force o the auld saw "The cannie Scot is weill-cryit: he cannie think, he cannie speik, he cannie express hissel". A reputatioun fur inartieculacie is bad eneuch, bot it is nae wunner whan the Scot hes tae be artieculat in anither's wey; an wan o the problems is the lack o screivit airgumentatioun in his ain leid. Weill, this is a shot at that, an attemp tae supply a wee bit o a thing, a *contributioun,* tae whit the Scots ar ment tae be quite guid at, exposietioun an airgument

Itherwise, this experiment is somthin at ithers micht follow up, fur we need mair attempts an monie mair shots gin oor leid is tae hae a chance tae tak back its fu range. I'm glad tae hae lerrit a whein Scots, and I am richt glad tae see sae muckle poetrie an owersets o Homer an the Bible, fur ensample. Bot mair maun be duine, or I hae leirit anerlie hauf a leid, wi the virr an couthie expressioun bot nae precisioun. Musardrie, sang an swearin ar aa gey weill, bot thai dinna get a toung back in fettle bi thairsels.

James Miller

Til R.L.S.

Ee got id wrong aboot Week, ma loon;
'e meanest o man's toons on e baldest o God's beiys.'
Yon wisna e richt thing til say;
ee didna ken e fowk, ee didna ken wir weiys
at first. An ee wis noor cut oot
til be an engineer lek your faither's faither
at pit a lichthoose on e Skerries.
No, we ken at ee wid raither
traivel through Reekie's hotchan wynds
and at Poetry's well sit doon and take your dram.
Bit we ken as weel at fan ee left
e north and took e long road hom
at amang your tulgeans wis memories
o e sea's work, o boats an wrecks, and maybe a man caad Gunn
at we'd meet again on a fantasy island.
So, fan aa is said and done,
ee micht be wishan, Tusitala,
at ee could tak your pen and yon line strick oot;
but ye canna; and we widna
want ee til cheinge id now, I doot.

*Robert Louis Stevenson spent a few weeks in Wick in 1868, part of his
brief attempt to learn civil engineering. In an essay, he wrote
disparagingly about the northern town.*

Autumn

In e back end e year fan a cowld win flings
frush whisperan fanns o e season's growth
til crunch ablow ma feet, and shortenan days
put a tichtnan branks on summer's scowth,

e thocht o fit I hevna deen
lies thick lek haar in ma mind,
obscuran far I thocht I's makan for;
then I haud on, wait for time til synd

oot misthocht; for a sharp, ree, cleansan frost
fan e moon, a lowan lantern, birls intil sicht,
scatteran siller sparks on nicht's black hearth,
kindlan an ailass o white, uncanny licht.

Snapshot O Keiss

A reegbon o reefs
spires an lums
tween hill an braeheid

tiltan afore e gale
stern til e westard
anchored til e hard

lapped roond wi parks
stitched wi diks,
a weave o fences

ranks o creels,
a caakane o maas
ower Bremner's haven

ston set on ston
wi sweit and love,
a declaration

Lookan North Fae Lossie

Fifty mile o blue-grey sea atween me
and e blue kenspeckle ridge o lan
far smaa'er hills peiy coort til Morven

An airt knotted roond wi wattled lace
an airt gien ower til maas and men
at kent e very waves by name

In e owld photos o wir memory
tan sails flick lek swallows' wings
and every geo is planted thick wi masts

A smirr o rain washes oot e hills
and in e blue-grey vacancy o sea
a scarlet maple leaf laments wir skailt inheritance

*In the spring of 1995, many Scottish fishermen flew the Canadian flag to
show their solidarity in the dispute over Alantic fishing rights between
Spain and Canada.*

London, Easter 1995

In iss April-sunlit southern city,
ower beeg for hids ain good, I stan on stons
at cam sooth afore me, a century ago
in a schooner's howld, e thin-sliced bons
o Caithness, shipped til lie wi slate and brick
in a lithic exile; while e pentatonic song
o a Chinese band fills Covent Garden
wi sounds at seem til be takkan long
for bamboo-cled braes; and a loon –
heid doon, maybe twenty, canna be mair –
sits in a tulter o claes, in e private exile
o poverty, rachlan til fecht off despair
on Hungerford Bridge – cowld ston
ablow him, and Thames's solemn reach,
and fowk pressan past lek anither tide
cerryan naethane, naethane, til beach
o e teem barren shore o his howp.
Flocks o tourists settle, tak off again,
bricht birds o passage, steeran aboot
wi siller til spend and sichts til hain.
Id seems we're aa ootcasts here in
iss toon far I bade an wrocht echt year
and hev come back til now, aa adrift,
far fae hom, flotsam washed in here.

Letter Til A Past Love

E cannel-lowe at blins a moch's great een
hes no deceit in mind. E thocht, if thocht
is ere at all, lies aa wi them at's keen
til win e flichteran prize. At's how we wrocht,
and lek e moch, we baith flew eidently,
each ain strecht til his or her bricht fate,
and fell, wi fluttran wings and herts in ecstasy,
and lay egither as if time idsel would wait,
stan still for us, but maybe we should hev kent
it couldna last. E flaman lowe burnt doon.
We ken there wis nae hairm in wir intent
and though e pairtane wis for us a stoon,
there's solace yit and joy in memory o ee
And e howp at ee could write e same til me.

Gordon Meade

The Great Northern Diver

I have always wondered
What it would have been like
To have been born
A Great Northern Diver.

In the early days
Of my imaginings I feared
I might not have been able
To hold my breath long enough
To have seen anything of interest
Beneath the surface of the waves.

Latterly, however,
I am more concerned
I may no longer be able
To remain afloat long enough
In order to breathe.

Lion's Mane Jellyfish

If the sun went through
The same sorts of phases as the moon,
These would represent the dark.

Dotted along Shell Bay,
Over a dozen of them, the colour
Of dried blood, are waiting to die,
Or are already dead.

Sprawled across the sand,
These creatures of the ocean found
Their Waterloo on land.

They'll stay until the next
Tide comes. Reading them their lack
Of rights, like some demented policeman,
He'll move them further on.

Aristotle and Socrates

Two barn owls in a cage: one flying,
Rattling its bars on landing; the other,
Settled in a corner, perfecting its rage.
What has come between them is a dead mouse.

It lies on the same spot where it landed,
When it was thrown in by the owls' keeper
Over an hour ago. Neither bird will sink so
Low as to pick it up and eat it. One hunts

A patchwork of shadows thrown by the sun
On the cage's blank wall; the other dreams
Up a moonrise through half-closed eyes; while
The mouse festers silently on the floor.

MacDuff, On a Friday Night in June

Here, the harbour mouth is just
Too narrow, as if the trawlers, steadying
Themselves for an escape, are actually
Trapped like ships in bottles.

From the lounge bar of a deserted hotel
The sea looks reasonably calm, but no more
Than two hundred yards from the end of the pier,
Ocean Challenger dips and bobs, momentarily
Disappears. She is shadow-boxing with the swell,
Ducking and diving, weaving out and in, taking
Each breaking wave full on the chin.

In under an hour from now, when she
Can see nothing but water, I'll stand
In a renovated church, beneath the shadow
Of the cross, and read some poems, each one
Stolen from the bottom of the sea.

The Ice Factory

This is where water is transformed
Into ice, fashioned into blocks, and smashed,
Loaded into a cement mixer, and driven
To the quay. There, it will be transferred
Into the hold of a trawler, and used
As a preservative, to keep dead fish fresh,
To anaesthetize the wounds of the sea.

The Sea
for Sophie

It comes in, rushing,
too busy to stop for anyone,
or anything.

Sand is nothing to it;
so easily brushed aside. Rock presents
more of a problem;

but it too, in time,
will be reformed, eroded, washed away. Everyday
the sea changes everything;

both itself,
and the coastline, which tries to contain it. Remain
by its edges long enough,

and you too,
will be remade; your lips taste of salt, your hair
develop curls you thought

impossible,
and your eyes water at the slightest mention
of the word - *Wave.*

Neil McNeil

Clonahan at Dawn

Peering through Calum's cracked oak barn door
his eyes caught the doves faint as cobwebs
in flight like blobs of ghost light.

He opened the door, shuffled across the stone floor
through dust from the harvests of centuries
weighed down by aeons of being alone

he was as sure as ever he'd left no trace.
Clonahan ransacked his memory.
Yes! It had been the same in the Sahara.

And in the sloped streets of San Francisco
or further back when he'd tracked lost tribes in Nevada.
His frantic scan stirred dust, sand, straw.

He'd never known from what seed he'd grown.
No one would ever tell of the chilled and chilling cell
drawn out of cities, ashes, crushed stone and blood.

He yelled! The doves fled.
Clonahan remembered he'd left
His mark on the moon.

The Assassination of Sol

Once upon a time long long ago
You used to worry about ravens
Pecking out the eyes, having a go
At the living lamb.

But now you know who I am
You understand all things from stars to protons
Are up for grabs.

It will take roughly centuries.
The next step after we thoroughly kill the sun
Is how to get rid of the body.

Of course we can't just leave the carcass
Adrift in the sky with them out here asking us why.
That's the bare bones of it.

The Night Nixon Resigned

It was something of an event.
Others called it a concert lecture
by John Cage
with time to listen
and not listen.
With silence and silence
arranged for no sleep.

There is a special structure of silence in a theatre's
wing and burglar's soles.

From side to side of the auditorium
letters
notes
words
silences

Is the concert taped?
Is the lecture?
Are silences the same played back?

Curtains.
The performer bows out

We are left with echoes, space.
Filled by one word which was only a place
until infamous.

Planet

Far out at the outer limit
innocent, full of wonder
iridescent, full of measure
greater than the sum of smaller
histories, pre-galactic, pre-solar,

this planet looks a bit pot-bellied.
Pear shaped. Lumpish. Fat at one end.
Not the perfect spherical curvature
legend has tethered in time.

Our metaphors for atoms have become
dirt too hot to handle.
Dirt that digs through closed seams
of where we seek shelter or our homes.

Digs through this. My own foil suit and poem.

Song for Wang Pi

Tonight there is an eclipse
of the moon.
In each child
woman
man
What has come
has also gone.

When there are no bonds
we remain together
inside. In speech
false words
come and go.

As did Tu Fu and Li Po
you and I
ferry to and fro
drown at sea
like waves running madly
when squeezed into this small space
of I.

In this close proximity,
kissing point of earth and sky
tears drop from one
of nine broken moons.

Tu Fu's poems speak of changes,
my pibroch melts in my pipe.
Is there a big enough ceol mor
for the crushed harmonics of Beijing?

Cathy Wright

And Then We Sever

The Ayrshire resort of Kilgillan, golden-sanded pleasure-town and second home to Burns, has recently become the teen death capital of Scotland. In separate incidents, two boys were stabbed during fights in the High Street after closing time; a fourteen-year-old joyrider crashed into a bollard and died in hospital; and in the space of three months, two young girls have died in the same nightclub. The furious boredom of the small town has erupted with a vengeance. Or perhaps Kilgillan is jealous of its city neighbours, and must swallow a certain number of its own young?

So the more excitable local, and now even national, papers are saying. Mary thinks it's a load of old crap. Idiots from the local schemes speed in a stolen car, or get shit-faced, pick a fight and get themselves killed – sad, but hardly astonishing. Or some daft cow takes pills from a stranger, could be drain-cleaner for all she knows, and swallows them right down – then it's all the Council's fault, and they should be shutting down Heaven. There have been pictures of Heaven in the papers – they've made it look like Castle Dracula, all looming façades and lowering skies and gun-metal seas. Usually captioned like *Dying To Get To Heaven?* What bollocks.

In reality Heaven is just tacky-looking – an ex-Seventies warehouse, hideous yellow-grey concrete, standing alone on the sea-front as if the nice B&B's don't want to rub shoulders with it. Inside isn't much better. But the alternative is Sanjay's on the High Street, full of men in suits trying to pick up young girls, which calls itself a wine bar though the wine tastes like vinegar. It's disgusting, but Mary has to tell her Mum that's where she goes, nowadays. Mum would blow a gasket if she thought Mary was at Heaven.

Mary has to get out of this town. She and her friends say it to each other all the time but she is starting to mean it now. She can't take much more of the small-town mentality, which regards her with suspicion because she is a teenager. She can't stand the lack of clothes shops, book shops, record shops, any shops except tourist kitsch shops. Most of all she can't stand the omnipresence of Robert Burns, Land O'Burns, the Burns monument, his doe-eyed face peering down at her from every window. Mary has been studying him in First Year English at Kilgillan College, and she's been finding out the truth about the Ploughman Poet. "That stuff about being a man of the people, and he was the *darling* of the Edinburgh aristocracy," she fumes to her father, "not to mention a hypocritical, two-faced misogynist."

"I always thought he liked women," her father says. "He got through enough of them."

"Exactly – he didn't *like* them, did he? He just fathered another baby, wrote them a poem and he was off."

"Ah, but they seemed to like him that way," her father says, winking at her mother. Mary boils with rage.

Mary's escape plan is beginning to take shape. She has her eye on Glasgow. Glasgow, city of clubs and nightlife, where you can buy CD's at midnight and cappuccino at 3 a.m. Glasgow, where Wednesday half-closing is nothing but a joke. Mary reckons that after a year at Kilgillan College she can get a transfer to one of the Glasgow universities – she may have to repeat First Year, which will mean no grant, but she'll think about that later. She has to escape from her mother's oppressive worrying, and her Dad getting drunk and singing the songs Burns wrote for his sexual victims – sometimes he even sings *Sweet Highland Mary*, and Mary has to leave the room.

That's the long-term escape plan. The short-term involves Saturday nights out with friends, down the Union or (now that's been closed down due to asbestos in the roof) Heaven. She'll have a few drinks, or maybe something a bit stronger, nothing excessive. Not that she tells her mother this – Mum would go absolutely ballistic. This infuriates Mary, because doesn't her mother smoke? *And* she drinks – does she think Mary can't see what state she's in when she comes back from the Police Social? But when Mary wants to take something different, non-respectable, something (above all) non-taxable, Mum just freaks. It's ridiculous. And it's not like Mary's stupid about it – she only takes anything from her mate Stu, who's in Third Year at College (hardly a pusher) who knows exactly what's in all his stuff. When she takes a pill she *knows* what's happening to her insides, which is more than her Dad can say when he opens a bottle of whisky.

So tonight she gets dressed without a care in the world. She puts on her black leggings, the ones that make her thighs look nice and thin, and then her ankh pendant, which as an afterthought she tucks inside her top until she gets outside (after the stupid jokes her Dad made about it last time). She is going to meet her College friends Holly and Sue and Alison. Real friends, they are, not like the bitchy backstabbing gang at school, friends she doesn't have to compete with, although she is happily aware that some people think she's the best-looking of the four. Real mates. She sings to herself as she thinks about them, brushing her long red hair.

Then on with her jacket, and down the stairs and out. Her parents detain her for a while. Who will she be with? When will she be back? This used to annoy Mary, but now she thinks they're a bit pathetic – just because they've got nothing better to do on Saturday night but watch telly. She is starting to realise how little power they have over her, and can afford to be generous. Dad gives her money for a taxi home, which she doesn't like to tell him will probably be spent on a kebab – she walks most of the way home with Alison, and besides, what's going to happen to her *here?*

Then out, and away! She meets the others at Sanjay's. The skies are still lilac beyond the picture windows, but the bar is already crowded. The girls debate whether to stay here for a few drinks, but the men in suits are already beginning to stare. When one of them tries to chat up Sue, they decide to go straight on to Heaven.

By the time they walk to the sea-front the sky is dark, and Heaven is lit up like a mosque. A garish, ugly concrete mosque maybe – but as the girls join the crowds of people trooping towards it, they begin to feel the excitement. A bunch of schemey-looking lads are running and pushing along the sea-wall, showing off for the girls with them. Mary and Holly and Sue and

Alison give them a wide berth, but they still start to catch the mood – by the time they enter Heaven's concrete forecourt, and the first booming rhythm of the club reaches them, they are marching and swaying in time.

Heaven's grubby foyer is a mass of security. Men with black teeshirts and Hitler complexes shout and push at the boys in front of Mary; one of them gives some lip so they all get searched. Mary and her friends keep quiet and besides, they're girls, so they only get a handbag search. Papered round the hallway are yellow handbills warning of the Dangers of Drugs. Then they pay for their tickets, seems like more every time; then they move on to the cloakroom, where a sour-faced female hangs up their coats and flings raffle tickets at them for a further 20p. It's more like Immigration Control at Heathrow than the entrance to a nightclub. "Are we really paying for this abuse," Mary says loudly and the other three laugh. They are trying to be cool, for they can hear the thumping rhythm from the next room now, like a salmon can feel the sea – and their hearts give a great leap, as they never fail to do, as they push open the swing doors and move into the blackness beyond.

In natural light, Heaven's interior is scabby beyond belief. But the blackness, the whirling strobes, the crowd and the music are not just transforming but transporting; a good club is like a shift in dimension. If the fire doors were to open at the height of the evening, and the crowds propelled out into the car-park, they would be amazed to find themselves still in Kilgillan.

The entrance to Heaven is a level above the main hallway, with access to the dancefloor down a metal staircase. This gives the Council Health and Safety something else to complain about – and a great view of the dancefloor to the newcomers. It's early in the night; but 'No Limits' is on, so the dancefloor is already a heaving mass, swept by spotlights. Mary and her friends descend to the floor, squeezing past the loiterers on the stairs, personal space forgotten. Mary's eye is caught by someone in white, with dark, dark hair – but when she looks again she is at ground level, and a forest of heads has sprouted up around her. Her friends behind her are pressing forward onto the dancefloor. She lets herself be carried into the dance.

After a while they break to get a drink. Alison, who's turning into a right hardcore bitch these days, is already on the lookout for Stu, but the others are content to pace themselves. They push through the sweaty crush around the bar, Mary in the lead as she's the tallest – and there, glowing in the dark, she sees him again. He is all in white, white sweat-top and trousers; his skin is fair but his hair is black and sleek. He is tall, taller than Mary, and quite broad, but not fat, not fat at all.

"Wow, Keanu Reeves," says Holly, and at that Mary knows she must get him, must must must. But they're all gaping at him like idiots: Mary firmly leads the way to the bar. But by the time she looks round again, he's gone.

The other three are giggling, which shows how little they care about him, really. Mary gets in a round, then packs her friends off to look for a table while she goes to the loo. She may never find them again, but doesn't care. She needs to think. She stares at herself in the bathroom mirror, surrounded by clouds of hairspray, and thinks hard. But then she doesn't have to think any more because when she emerges from the toilets, there he is.

He smiles at her, a bit shyly she thinks. His eyes are as dark as his hair, like chocolate. His fair skin is lightly freckled. She has never seen freckles as attractive before, but now she thinks they're beautiful. He holds out his hand, and she takes it. They seem to understand one another perfectly. He leads her out onto the dancefloor. They push through the crowd. His hand is hot and dry. Mary hopes hers isn't sweating too much. Her knuckles brush the back of his leg through the soft fabric of his clothes.

They reach a small space in the crowd and he turns to face her. He is so close she can feel his heat. M-People come on, and the space around them tightens as people surge onto the dancefloor. Mary is pushed even closer to him. They start to dance. Mary can hardly look at him. Her heart is hammering. She's never been in love before – she's not sure if she can bear it.

Two girls in identical black bodysuits are gyrating frantically, unsmilingly, beside her. Casually, as if they're eating Tic-Tacs, they dry-swallow a capsule each. Mary looks at him and smiles to show she's cool about this, and what's more, when *she* does it she manages to look like she's having fun. Perhaps he pulls the smile as an invitation, for he takes two pills from his pocket. He takes Mary's hand so he can tip one of them into her palm. The pills are small and white and chalky, no more exciting than aspirin. Mary doesn't care. When he swallows his, she gulps down hers.

Now they are intimate, united by illegal activity. Mary becomes bolder, and favours him with a dazzling smile, and he puts his hands on her waist. She meshes her fingers behind his neck, and they dance like that, barely touching, till the end of the record. Another record passes, and another. They still haven't spoken. They don't know each other's names. Mary is beginning to realise that they are above such things – other people have to work at it, chat and buy drinks and tell each other lies. But they only have to dance. They have found one another. Mary has never been so happy.

She is conscious after a while that Alison, Holly and Sue are dancing behind her. Alison tries to speak to her, but Mary just smiles and shakes her head. She wishes they wouldn't waste their time worrying about her. She wishes, for that matter, they wouldn't waste their time dancing with each other. They should be off looking for love. She wants them to be as happy as she is – she wants to share it with the whole world. Cynical bitches though her friends are – like she used to be! – she's sure she can make them understand. But when she turns back to explain it to them, they are gone.

She turns back to him, and his face is close to hers. Their lips brush. She can smell aftershave and clean sweat. She has never smelled anything so good. She never knew how taste and smell could give the purest joy. But then he goes to speak – perhaps to ask her name? He'll break the spell! She presses her fingers over his mouth. He seems to understand, and they draw apart and continue the dance. Half the night passes. Several times he kisses her again, each time more urgently, but Mary knows there is no hurry. Of course he is impetuous – she loves him for it! But they have all the time in the world. This is only the beginning.

Mary hears an anxious voice at her elbow, and there is Sue. Gorgeous little Sue, with her short black hair, coffee-cream skin and dark eyes, which now look so worried. Of all of them, Sue might understand most readily. Mary tries to draw her towards them, into their circle of happiness. But Sue pulls away – she is saying something, but Mary can't make it out. Mary tries to tell her this, but Sue can't seem to hear her either, just looks at her blankly.

Mary suddenly spots her friend Stu beyond Sue's shoulder. She remembers when she needed Stu's little pills to get high, before love came and swept all that away. Sweat spills into her eyes like summer rain. Mary laughs for the sheer joy of it – she lets go of her lover and whirls like an ice-dancer, red hair fanning out around her, droplets of sweat splashing into his face. The Shaman are playing, and she moves to the primeval rhythm, laughing at the magic that music and scent and taste and love have created.

Then a wave of heat hits her, dry as a desert wind. Her stomach starts to cramp. She tries to say something but her mouth is parched. She slides helplessly to the floor, down among the stomping feet. Her head bangs on the hard tiles. Her whole body is shaking, she can't stop it, even though she is so terribly hot. Voices babble, the music thuds tunelessly on, she can feel it through her aching head.

She lies on her back, looking up into flashing lights, surrounded by towering hot bodies. She can't see white clothes dark eyes and hair anywhere, but maybe he is standing behind her. That face mooning down to her might be Sue's. She can't see very well anyway. For some reason she is thinking of Burns's Highland Mary, dead in childbirth – nineteen and so alive and yet dying, the Poet's child bursting out of her; dying from too much life.

Mary begins to bleed.

Within hours, Kilgillan is the biggest media event since Dunblane. When the ambulance comes for Mary's poor dehydrated body, the first reporter is right behind it – by next morning Kilgillan has gone national. Two rare deaths could be coincidence, everyone reckons, but three is an epidemic.

At once the search is on for a scapegoat. The boy in white seen with Mary is a hot favourite, but since no-one can identify him and he has declined to come forward, he is soon abandoned in favour of Heaven itself.

The fences around the nightclub are reinforced to withstand local anger. Nevertheless a gang of children, Mary's cousin among them, manage to break through. They light a fire in the car park, and chant verses they have invented or culled from horror films; they have to leave when Mary's cousin starts to cry, but they count the exorcism a success. Perhaps they are right, because the District Council closes Heaven the next week. Heaven is boarded up, falls prey to neglect and savage vandalism, and is soon demolished to make way for a MacDonald's.

Mary's funeral is shielded from the cameras as much as possible. It is well-attended. Her mother wants *Unchained Melody* to be played, because Mary always liked it. But her father is a traditionalist, and chooses Robert Burns –

Ae fond kiss, and then we sever!
Ae fareweel, and then forever!
Deep in heart-wrung tears I'll pledge thee!
Warring sighs and groans I'll wage thee!

The Mouth of the Ocean

Hugh Clark Small

The ocean doesn't really have a mouth. It has ragged white teeth. Teeth that crack open on the rocky shoreline. It has foamy white spittle too. Rabid dog ocean. All the foam puddles collect in the grey basins; stranded until the next big breaker collects them. Has it got a tongue? If it has, it must be salty and unquenchable. All the yarns and shanties it spins.

Serpentine has a mouth. But she doesn't really have an ocean. Not any more. Her ragged white teeth are chattering with the cold. Her tail is wrapped around her torso to keep the elements at bay. The mermaid on the rock: Serpentine is her name.

Me? I am the boy with luminous feet. I'm paddling in the shallow, within earshot, within biting distance. Naked from the ankles up. Beneath the water, the yellowy-green glint of my luminous feet. They need soothing; they've been glowing too brightly of late. Impossible to sleep because of the unyielding glare. Even now, Serpentine is knitting me a pair of socks made from seaweed; the thickest strands of seaweed. They should extinguish the glow. She hopes.

She shivers and tail flinches, casts on and off; click, click, click go the driftwood needles. Humming a tune with her siren voice sometimes. She attracts nothing. No Fish = No Ships. Had their chips, so to speak. Her breasts are saggy and her whelk nipples droop low. But the starfish that grows from her forehead still looks good. Yes, Serpentine is the girl for me. She is the girl for the boy with luminous feet. We are an odd couple.

When I say there are no fish, I exaggerate. There are a few still. Since the shipping embargo, they even prosper and grow. The shoals are multiplying. As if to verify this, hundreds of tiny minnows congregate round the phosphorescence of my feet. Moths to a flame. They are instantly repelled by the smell. Ships to a lighthouse.

The chief gull, Gulliver, told Serpentine that the Bird Meeting had even sanctioned a higher catch quota. Good news – Serpentine dreamt that night of the good old days. Hundreds of fishing boats, slouching low with their gluttonous hauls, lured towards our rock by her enchanted singing. How she would feast on the wreckage. But it was only a fanciful dream. For she remembered how my luminous feet warned them off. Moths to a flame. Ships to a lighthouse. Attraction and repulsion.

Now I'm on the rock beside her. I tickle her tail a little and she smiles brightly. Her scales are dry, so I stroke my still-wet feet over the chameleon-like repeating pattern. She has beautiful scales. The best I've seen on a mermaid. She sings beautiful scales too. Higher and higher until they become inaudible. How do I know they still exist? Because the gulls come to listen. They cock their heads affectionately, their red and yellow hooked bills half-open in wonder. Gulliver leads the screech of approval when she ceases, then they all fly off in a squadron of V-shapes. They never shit on our rock. We never shit in their sea. Shit has never been a

Mike Spring's illustration

mark of respect.

Serpentine puts her driftwood needles down and takes up my luminous feet in her hands. She studies them, rubs them, kisses them. She has no sense of smell, but a keen awareness of sensation. Her little finger maps its way over my soles. I giggle. She sucks my toes, one by one. The nails sparkle; bright, white diamonds. I am excited. The pointless thrill of the eunuch. My finger gently circles a whelk. Her starfish gyrates. Yes, we are a very odd couple.

Maybe Serpentine's mouth is the true mouth of the ocean. Her ragged white teeth more vicious than the breakers. Flesh-eaters both. She has songs to lure, more powerful than any heart-warming shanty. The Baltic chill whistles; the mouth of the sky. Serpentine resumes her click, click, clicking. She's going to knit us some seaweed jerseys next. Yes, I agree, the climate is definitely changing for the worse. We will clothe ourselves in nature, camouflage our bodies from the elements.

The chief gull swoops low and screeches excitedly. Alas, I still cannot understand his language. Serpentine is my sole interpreter. She drops the needles at Gulliver's news and lets out an ultrasonic cry. What is it? This isolation kills me. I must calm her. Calm, calm, be calm, Serpentine. Tell me the news.

A Ship.

Yes, a ship. the gulls are following it even now. It is a hungry ship. A lone hunter. Fat from its catch, but still eating. An obese ship let loose on a fresh banquet. A solitary thief on the ocean. The mouth of the ocean. Yes, maybe the ocean does have a mouth after all; a man-made mouth. A roving mouth with ragged white teeth, bobbing, biting and chewing at everything in its path.

My luminous feet emit an over-excitable glow. Serpentine looks alarmed. Gulliver flies off to join the feast. Dusk is falling fast; soon my feet will become a lighthouse again – Serpentine resolves something within, picks up the needles and works furiously at her task.

My seaweed socks are a good fit. I stand tall and naked, admiring them from above. Admiring them, although I cannot see them. Yes, they work. Serpentine is ecstatic. She starts to sing songs of melancholy and enchant-ment. Inside, she is churning with the anticipation of an old hunger. There is a bright light after all. Not from my feet, but from the horizon. The smooth circumference at the edge of our very odd world. The sky and sea are divided by the indefinable line we have never touched. The white light; glowing, approaching, gullible. The gulls shriek secrets down the wind. There is no moon. No moon; no face to witness the carnage, the wreckage, the ironic comeuppance from the mouth of the ocean. Not the ocean's mouth, but Serpentine's.

I am happy for her. Happy that her vocation is being realised. She sings for her supper. Me? I am the boy with luminous feet, a fish out of water wherever I go. Now my sole attributes are masked, invisible. I shuffle off towards the back of our rock. The going is tough. I no longer have the light to guide me. I clamber over slippery, moist stone. Waves lap against the shoreline. A rhythm in the darkness, over which, Serpentine spins a spider's web of harmonies. Eerie in the pitch black, even for one who has kissed the mouth from which they flood. The ocean's mouth.

As the fly draws closer, I retract further. I sit near the Southern cave entrance, waiting for the walrus to ask me in. But he is a deaf old mammal now and is usually made aware of me by my glow. I consider removing one of my socks. Just as I'm about to yield to the temptation, I hear the rough growl of his voice from within. I whisper down into the cavernous echo chamber and he growls back in response. I understand walrus growl far better than seagull shriek. Admittedly, our conversation is often rudimentary.

Once inside, I dare to remove my seaweed socks. The sudden glare is blinding. A golden yellow glow throws black shadows into every cranny. The walrus, startled, growls disapprovingly at the shock of the illumination. I apologise profusely before telling him the great news. Yes, yes, he growls, the gulls are free with their gossip. And what of the ship's advancement?

No sooner does he ask me this, than an almighty crash thunders through the very bowels of the rock. The mouth of the ocean has bitten. Gull shrieks drown out human screams. Serpentine ceases to sing beautiful harmonies. Now she taunts with violent caterwauling; musical bile. The walrus winces. My luminous feet dull from an inner numbness. We sit in silence with our minds full of vivid pictures. We sit like this, it seems, for ever and ever.

There is a strong smell of seaweed in my nostrils. I wake early, still in the cave, though the walrus has gone. My socks are on my hands. My hands have been shielding my eyes all through sleep. Don't let the nightmares in. My feet are healthy-looking beacons. They lead me to the cave entrance, from which, I survey the Southern seascape. Calm and blue and endless. I walk into the shallow, the ocean's energy rising up inside me, filling me with calm, blue, endless thoughts. Southern thoughts.

The Northern end looks much the same, save for the rock broken carcass of shipwreck lapping gently on the beach. Serpentine is fat today. She has been gorging all through the night. But I know where she hides her larder. She'll be letting the gulls pick now.

She looks quite maternal with her driftwood needles, smiles on my arrival and tells me she's starting the seaweed jerseys. I notice some blood red on the ragged white teeth in the mouth of the ocean. I taste it in her morning kiss. Her tail swishes contentedly, her whelks enlarged and proud, her starfish brow smooth as the sea. I look down at my luminous feet, my eunuch's groin, the seaweed socks still on my hands. Yes, I admit, we are a very odd couple.

Comrade Hat

Pippa Stuart

On a dreary mid-winter morning in the Christian Centre for the unemployed and down-and-outs the Hat first appeared. The door of the dining room was pushed slowly open and in it came, this remarkable greenish-black hat with a high dome of a crown and amazingly curled brim, the kind of head-gear belonging to better days and a better life. Its owner, for it had an owner and didn't wander in on its own right, wore a frayed black coat with dangling buttons. He had a cadaverous face, blue with cold. He hesitated, looking around him timidly, then headed for what we claimed as our table.

Round it sat Big John, barely five feet, old Meggie who remembered distant days of youth, mean-faced Liz, hard as a nail, smoking like a furnace, Sam, with his jaw-shaking stammer and Timmy who never spoke. If he did a silence fell: *Hear Timmy!* Ginger-headed Padd seldom sat with us, preferring to prowl about restlessly on the outskirts, sniffing out trouble. It was impossible to have secrets here, we knew the worst of one another. When Padd heard what I had been he gave his most fiendish cackle: "Here's our Holy Father, come to take confession. Bless us, Holy Father, we're in need for blessings." The more he sneered the quieter I grew and in the end he gave up baiting me, but I knew that if he could ever hurt me he would.

We were all there now, this Monday morning, slumped over our porridge, greasy sausages and black pudding, washed down with stewed tea from the giant urn. We hated the Christian centre that fed us, resented the high-minded, self-righteous ladies of the Kirk who served us, above all we loathed the monotony and hopelessness of Monday mornings. Now we stared, fascinated, at the Hat. Its wearer, after more hesitation, sat down on the chair looked on as Padd's. He laid his hat on the floor beside him, patting it as if it were some pet puss.

"The name's Digby", he began in a cracked, high-pitched wheezing voice with no trace of our local accent. "Good Lord, hear him, he talks posh", came from Padd. "Some hat. La di da." The newcomer didn't seem to hear the taunt. "You're surely come down in the world", said Big John. "What did you do?" Liz asked. "I was in the service, what's called a butler." "What's that?" demanded Meggie. "A b-b-butler!" Sam exclaimed, impressed. "I saw an advertisement: 'Wanted reliable man; interview necessary.' I needed a hat for that, and in the next shop window noticed the sign: 'Genuine reductions.' There it was, sitting on a shelf, this very hat. From the first it seemed to be speaking to me: 'Take me, no, not that one never! TAKE ME!' The moment I touched the brim I knew it was the hat for me."

Unlike Timmy, Digby talked. Talk flowed from him. There had never before been anyone like him in the centre. And all the time he was mopping up the yolk of egg with his bread – nibble, nibble, not our usual munch crunch guzzle gulp – and all the time smiling around as warily, nervously, as if afraid of being buffed. Some colour was coming back to his face.

"Well, what next?" Liz demanded impatiently. "What next? I set the hat on my head. 'If I may say so', the salesman said. 'It suits your style'." "La di da," Padd repeated but we ignored him. "He took off half the price for the lining was greasy, shop-soiled, he called it." "Was your hat on at the interview?" Meggie insisted. She had worn the same moth-eaten woollen bonnet for years. "Most certainly," said Digby. "Also my father's old coat, this very one, well-brushed and the buttons sewn on tight." "La di da", sneered Padd. Timmy suddenly sat up. "Wheest!" he said. "Ssh-ssh-ut up P-Padd", Sam brought out. Padd glared. He was furious that this newcomer should take over his role as the chief actor in the human comedy of the Centre.

Each day Digby added more details. "I wore white gloves to serve at table," he told us. "Yes. And a red waistcoat. All the talk I heard. Oh, the times we've had, Comrade Hat and I! Once there was a duke, another time even a lord." "And the Queen?" Meggie suggested. "N-no, not the queen. There was a clean white tablecloth, tumblers all shining, no gobs of food left in the forks, plates washed for every course, the Master carving the roast beef, me asking 'Red or white, Sir?'" "D-did you w-wear your h-hat to serve?" "No, Sam, not to serve. On my day out I'd set it on my head – so! 'You look quite the gentleman, Digby,' the Master said, and when his wife was there she'd tell me 'I do love your hat, Digby. It's so expressive.'" "La di da, expressive", came from Padd along with a jealous glower.

Each morning when the Warden chased us out into the streets to wander about during the endless day, Digby could take up his tale. "If that hat could have spoken it would have warned me. I might still be there with my gloves and red waistcoat." "I'd like fine to have seen the red waistcoat", said Timmy. "T-timmy's getting talkative", said Sam. "If only I'd been warned!" Digby repeated. "What happened?" Big John asked. "It all began in the but-ler's pantry", said Digby. "I was tempted there." "Who tempted you?" "There were two voices – one said, 'Now, that's the last drop, Digby', very firm. But the other, a fine, low voice, whispered, 'Och, take another, you look cold, poor Digby. It won't do you any harm'. I was on the slippery slope."

We sat silent, waiting for the next instalment. "One night, since my hands weren't so steady, I spilt the soup over a guest, no, not the Duke. Then I did worse – I should have known better. You were supposed to stand behind the door, still as a stone, not a word out of you – but better than anything I loved to hear their talk. I went so far as to say to the Duke: 'If I may be so bold, Sir, I agree with every word you say.' That did it. 'It can't go on, Digby' the Master said. 'You've blotted your copy book. I warned you'. 'Just one more chance', I pleaded. 'There's no two chances in life. Mind it!' I picked up Comrade Hat. 'We're off to make our fortunes elsewhere,' I said. I was heart-broken to leave that fine life, the beautiful ladies, the way they tilted back their heads as they drank their wine, the fine way the gentlemen cut up their meat, not falling on it like dogs. You never heard them eating, not like here."

"What was your next job?" Liz asked. "It never turned up or if it did it never lasted." "Nothing lasts", said Liz. "Don't expect it to." "Life will improve", said Digby. "La di da," sneered Padd. I wanted to warn Digby to look out for Padd, never to trust him, to accept that in the Centre nothing did last, neither kindliness nor compassion, but he didn't believe me.

Sometimes at night I'd come on him sheltering up some grim close mouth. I knew it was Digby for I'd hear him muttering to himself, huddled up in the threadbare black coat, the hat pulled well down. "We've known better times, old Comrade, warmer beds", he would be repeating over and over. We often sat together on a bench in the railway station. "There you are, Digby, remembering how you poured the ruby red wine into those gleaming glasses." "Is it true that you were a priest?" "Years ago – forgot it all now. I forgot the order of the mass. Can you imagine me in my vestments, lifting up the chalice of wine, the holy water, flesh and blood of the Saviour? Better for the slippery slope to begin, if it has to begin, in the butler's pantry than at the altar. There's blasphemy I'm guilty of. Oh Digby, what a falling-off, we're fallen angels you and me, but my fall's deeper than yours. You're an innocent, Digby, a kind of Holy Fool. Lamb of God, wash away our sins, wash us clean in the blood of the Lamb – it comes back to me."

"Come on, move on you two", came a familiar voice – the Station Police. "You can't sleep there." Then, exasperated, "Have the pair of you ever done an honest day's work in your life?" Digby would stumble to his feet, shivering. "We make a pair", I'd say. "Oh Digby, *mon semblable, mon frère*. The degloved butler and the defrocked priest!" "You're my comrade along with Comrade Hat", Digby said in his rusty wheeze, coughing and spitting blood. "Perhaps Padd's not to be trusted, but I trust you." "Don't forget that nothing lasts in life except our sins." "I'll remember, Comrade."

Sometimes, over our first and last meal of the day, over our lumpy porridge and greasy sausages, Digby was full of hope, laying his hat on the table. "We're going to find a job, the pair of us. Just watch us." Padd was there, lurking in the background, listening, Satan in residence, bidding his time. He'd pay us all out – me for my "Lay off Digby, Padd!" – the other five for listening, spell-bound, to all his tales, but especially Digby himself for stealing his limelight.

One Monday morning in early February started badly. The snow turned to sleet, the roof leaked, the porridge stuck to the pot and was singed. The charitable ladies, the do-gooders, were more self-righteous than ever, the Warden was in bad humour. A sense of trouble brewing hung in the air, with Padd grinning his most diabolic grin. There was no sign of Digby.

All at once, as on that Monday morning months before, the door opened and in came the Hat and its owner. Like a barometer it measured the weather of its wearer. This day the brim was jaunty and Digby didn't slide in, he almost swaggered. "Comrade Hat and I have hopes", he began. "We might even have a job". No one looked up. They ignored him, sunk in their own misery. Who cared about Digby and his job?" "The porridge is b-burned b-black", Sam said. "I knew good porridge when I was young", Meggie said in her dismalest whine. "Well, you're not young now", said Liz sharply. "We only have to hear you girning away to know that."

Padd, like a serpent, chose that moment to strike. He had sniffed out that the mood had changed. He had waited and now his hour had come. He let out a low whoop, then he started to dance, skipping, swirling, and twirling, while along with his dance went a mocking chant. "Some butler! La di da!" Digby sat, shrinking, pale as a ghost, the hat on the table before him. "The times we've had, Comrade Hat!" Padd squealed. "Oh, the times!"

Then, as if evil had been unleashed into the stale air, one by one, we all joined in: "Brer Bonnet, Comrade Hat!" Hearing us, Padd's inventiveness increased. "Oh Comrade Hat, the slippery slope!" he squealed in a high falsetto wheeze, making a Digby voice, grimacing, transforming his face into a Digby face. And carried away by boredom, by Monday morning bleakness, we sang louder and louder. What could be funnier than Padd imitating Digby? Meggie and Liz screeched with laughter, tears streaming down their cheeks.

The nearer Padd came to Digby the more his agitation grew. It was like the baiting of some ancient ragged and shabby bear, tied to a stake, and we were all hungry dogs set on it, baying for blood. "Oh, the times we've had!" we all sang. "What's all the noise in here?" the Warden shouted, putting his head round the door. "Less of it." He quickly withdrew. The less he interfered the better, especially on a Monday morning. The ladies of good works had already fled.

Padd had now reached Digby and his hat. He snatched it up, waved it in the air, then pulled it down over his matted tangle of gingery hair. Digby tried to rise up but his legs gave way beneath him and he sank back on his chair. Padd went skipping off, round and round, until he stood beside the great tea urn. He turned on the tap, swept off the hat and filled it up with tea. Then in a flash he was back at our table and with a last "La di da" pulled the sodden hat down over Digby's head. It split, disintegrated, fell in tea-sodden snippets and slivers to the table, while the tea trickled down the folds and creases in Digby's ashen face. Slowly he gathered the remains of his hat together, turning the fragments over and over, help-lessly. Then he laid his head on the table and wept – a fearful stricken sound like a beast mourning the loss of its young.

There was silence. Digby's distress suddenly sobered us. "You should have left him alone, Padd", said Liz. "He l-loved h-his hat", Sam said. "It was as real as a dog or a cat, it could speak", said Timmy. In all the years we had known him this was the longest speech he had ever made.

Still without a word Digby rose up unsteadily, gathered together the remains of Comrade Hat and slowly left the dining room. He gave one backward glance and for a moment our eyes met. I can never forget the look he gave me. I wish I could. I thought: *Christ looked at Judas like that.* Everybody else vanished off from the Centre out into the bleak February day, until Padd and I were left alone. "Well, Holy Father," Padd sneared, leering all over his blotched face, "you didn't exactly hold out the hand of Christian love to dear Comrade Digby, did you?" "No, Padd, I didn't. You're bad for you enjoy evil and destroying a poor silly soul who never harmed you, but I'm worse, far worse than you for I never lifted a hand to help him and he expected that I would stand by him. Why I didn't is one of the riddles of our human condition. It's not likely that you've heard this before but here it is: *For the good that I would I do not, but the evil which I would not, that I do.* That's me, Padd."

For a long time I looked out for Digby but he never reappeared. He left something of himself behind in that grim Centre, however, for we kept remembering him. Timmy, after staring endlessly into space, would say, "I'd like fine to have seen yon red waistcoat", and Sam repeated, quoting Timmy "Y-yon h-hat – it w-was like a d-dog or c-cat. It as g-good as spoke t-to h-him." Meggie and John would mutter, "It wasn't fair what we did", and Liz, stubbing out another cigarette, would mutter vindictively, "Digby was decent. I hate Padd".

Padd himself somehow dwindled and dwindled. One morning he wasn't there with his battered face and evil leer, and that was the last of him. As for me, the memory of the look that Christ gave to my fellow betrayer would remain to haunt me to the end of my days.

Pàdraig Maclabhruinn

Fon a' Speur Trom

'Se a cheud bhalach le ball
Air an t-sràid a tha 'na ghaisgeach.

Chan eil seanalair am measg an t-sluaigh.
"Cha chuala mi càil, cha chuala mi càil"
Ars na calmain; is tha an sluagh a' feitheamh.

Chan eil ceò; chan eil teine;
Tha a' chaigealt fuar fhathast;
Is tha an sluagh a' feitheamh.

Under a Heavy Sky

The first boy with a ball on the street is a hero. There is no General among the people. "I heard nothing at all, I heard nothing at all" say the doves, and the people wait. There is no smoke, no fire; the hearth is cold yet, and the people wait.

An Ruaig

Bha mi a' coiseachd timcheall
A' chraobh air a' bhrugh
Nuair stad àm far a robh i.

Nuair bha mi leanabh
Cha robh eagal orm,
Ach chan urrain dhomh ceannsaich a-nis.
Coma leam dha do dhrùidheachd.

Bidh mi a siubhal
Air an rathad dìreach:
cha seallaidh mi
Air an linne donn.

Tha gliocas comasach
Aig an rèidio
Tha an telebhishean
Miòrbhuileach gu leor.

The Defeat

I was walking round the tree on the fairy mound when time stood still. When I was a child I was not afraid, but I cannot cope now. Enough of your magic! I shall walk the straight road: I shall not look into the brown pool. The radio has sufficient wisdom. The television is marvellous enough.

Mathair

Bha am falt aice cho soilleir
Ri bùrn aig meadhan-latha.
'Si a' chuimhne a bheir solas,
Ged tha e air falbh
As mo chuimhne an-dràsda.

Bidh cuimhne an t-solais agam
Ann an àros nan aosda
Nuair a theid mi dhachaidh.

Bha i ag ràdh gu robh
Am falt a' fàs gu beag
An-dèidh bàis, is gu robh
An solas a' fàs gu lan.

Mother

Her hair was as bright as fresh water at noon. Memory brings light, though it is slipping away now. I shall remember the light in the old folks' home, when I go to my long rest. She said that hair grows a little after death, and that the light grows great.

Am a' Bhruadair

Nuair bha mi ann an àm a' bhruadair
Bha an seabhag air a' gheug àrd;

Bha mo chridhe cho làn de ghaol
Ri madainn làn de òran nan eun.

Bha am bradan glic a' snàmh
Anns an lochan domhain.

Cha robh ainm orm:
'Se cànan na camhanaiche a bha agam.

Labhair na siantan, is bha mi gan tuigsinn
Leugh mi na reultan, is bha sin furasda.

Choisich mi ann an solas na grèine gun nàire.

Sheinn mi anns an driùchd deàrrsanta
Is cha robh mo chlarsach diòmhain.

Dreamtime

When I was in dreamtime, the hawk was on the high branch. My heart was as full of love as a morning full of birdsong. The wise salmon swam in the deep lochan. I was nameless: I spoke the tongue of dawn. The elements spoke and I heard. I read the stars, and it was easy. I walked in sunlight without shame. I sang in the bright dew, and my harp was not idle.

Le sacre du printemps

Una Flett

I have always imagined it in a very cold northern country, the first signs subliminal, a minute softening on an edge of ice, a drip of sound at a frozen waterfall, a hint of radiance shafting the still freezing dark. That first theme, the six pinched notes of the bassoon, an uneasy stirring in the womb-death of hibernation, pulling us shivering out of lairs and caves.

To me, the rites of spring were long before green appeared. The magic must catch exactly that first awe, the blind relief. But it's still nothing more than the flutter of a pulse. So the tribe must gather, and the priest must set us stamping and stamping, the force to be dragged from its feeble throb into the huge hopefulness of growth. The stamping pulls at the earth, wrenching at life itself. We drag spring out of the darkness. Only by our efforts and our blood will this huge cracking of the silence take place.

I never shared these images with anyone. Perhaps they grew out of the dancing. Perhaps others had other images, I don't know. When we performed this work I was beside myself with a queer excitement. When he was creating it he didn't explain anything, he just grouped us and occasionally bent our bodies to another shape, then showed us the movement. Mainly he insisted we *feel* our bodies differently. Not many generations have stood upright before you, he said. You can still smell the earth like animals, he said. I started to get a feel of what he wanted, and he singled me out to demonstrate. I stamped and crouched, a kind of cringing power in my body. Yes, that's it, he said.

But in the end the part of the Chosen Maiden went to Kati, taller and bolder-looking than me. I didn't mind as much as I'd expected. Why? Usually I wanted limelight as all dancers do. But not in "Sacre".

He worked very fast. In three weeks it was ready for the opening of the new season. There was no stage set and the costumes were nothing but minimal tunics. There was nothing but the music, the lights, and us.

He, of course, was the high priest – who else? – the one who finally chooses the sacrificial maiden. Sometimes, in a cold fit of detachment, right in the middle of a performance, I would so loathe him for having the power of life and death over us that I could have killed him there and then. One critic wrote that it was a dangerous work. Others called it obscene and brutalising. But one or two thought it was a work of genius.

He was pleased by all the reactions. He was even pleased the first night, making us stand our ground while the audience shouted and booed (there was a good core of "bravos", however) and even flung a few objects. We wanted the curtain to stay down, but he insisted that it go up again and again, acknowledging all this uproar as if it were the greatest ovation.

Afterwards, we celebrated, and he bought brandy and champagne and was extremely merry. He had his arms round me and Kati and was talking volubly, while the rest of us stayed silent, affected by that audience so rabidly angry.

He said, "Nijinsky would be proud of us, children. It was almost as chaotic as *his* opening of "Sacre" in Paris! You must never be afraid of a little shouting. It means far more than applause and bouquets – it means that you've actually struck sparks from the lumpen bourgeoisie. And *that* doesn't happen every Tuesday."

He was laughing. He had for once stepped out of his private god-world to celebrate with us, but I preferred him in his gaunt creative moods, or putting us through our classwork with hardly a word spoken. His face was a silent face, long and dark and expressive like a mime. And he spoke with his hands, whole sequences of steps he could sketch with those hands. We all knew his sign language, all dreaded when he made a kind of chopping movement, as if he wanted to cut off our rotten limbs for dancing so badly.

"Sacre" was a box-office success. People came to be scandalised, which in this age is quite an achievement. We did nothing overtly obscene on stage, yet it was orgiastic, grossly orgiastic. We felt it ourselves as we heaved and stamped. On 'good' nights we got it, this sense of a big coarse consummation, of some heavy-bodied bacchanalia, but with a purpose - oh yes, not just a release of feeling. I think this was what shocked people. It was not "catharsis", it was *how things happen,* how the wheel of being is made to turn. And is behind any revolution, assassination, terrorist act, or other enormity. They draw on *this* kind of energy. I'm sure of it.

I doubt if I could have coped with being the Chosen Maiden. Kati had a different temperament. She joked and chatted beforehand in the dressing-room, complained about the bruises from the rough-and-tumble of her sacrificial dance. Only when "five minutes please" was called, her face would go grey and shaky even through her make-up. In front of her was that appalling dance, in which she had to express terror like a long-drawn-out shriek, and all the time have her wits about her for the falls and lifts and all the tricks. I know, because he worked it out on me. But then he wanted Kati, taller and bolder-looking.

She never joked after the performance. As we walked back to our digs she would say distractedly, "I'll have to tell him. Tomorrow I'll tell him. I can't go through it again, I just can't. I *loathe* that ballet, I simply loathe it!"

But he always persuaded her, and the next time she would joke and chat in the dressing-room beforehand, sending the whole thing up.

I wanted to ask her, but never did, if she too felt my rage at him for having the power of life and death over us helpless girls huddled in a pack waiting to know who was for the axe. In my imagination I saw him wielding a black obsidian blade, such as the Aztecs used for their blood sacrifices. Of course there was nothing so crude as a weapon on stage. He sliced the Chosen Maiden with one slice of those formidable hands, those long flat hands whose blade-like qualities we dreaded in class.

One day he called us together unexpectedly after the performance. We went grumbling, wondering what had gone wrong. But it wasn't our dancing, it was something else. Unless we withdrew "Sacre" from the repertoire, he told us, we were going to lose the huge subsidy the town council provided us. This was shocking news. The council, we thought, were unconditionally on our side. But there had been threats and protests from the powers that be – the business community and some right-wing legal folk - that this public display of savagery must stop.

Of course, there was no question of complying. Could anyone imagine *him* backing down over anything? Let alone an attack on his beloved "Sacre"? We dispersed, grumbling quietly about the absurdity of risking our living because of this load of anthropological shit we had to perform every two or three nights. But in fact, after the first shock, no one took the matter seriously. Our reputation spread across two continents, we were part of the lustre of the town.

Three more performances took place, packed out. It seemed we'd called their bluff and got away with it. Then, on the morning of the second last performance we turned up at the theatre to find an extraordinary situation. *He* was on stage, ready to take class, in company with a stranger, a man with a civic look. And what he had to say, the man with the civic look, when we were all gathered (what a crew we were – old socks over stretch-satin tights, mangy pullovers belted tight, hair frizzing out of bright sweatbands, boys and girls alike) was that the theatre had been officially shut down. Therefore the orchestra had been dismissed and "Cancelled" notices put over all the main entrance.

When the man had gone, *he* told us to take our places at the barres. Not a word was said. He took the class, coldly and carefully as usual, and we sweated and our hearts thumped with exertion and unease, until finally –

"That's all, children. We had better conserve our energy for to-night."

We looked at each other in a kind of worried-sheep way. Somebody eventually said, rather low, "To-night?"

"Yes", he said courteously. "My plan is this. We stay here in the theatre the rest of the day. If we go out we'll never get back in – and at the usual time, we perform. To a tape."

"But who'll watch?" I blurted out.

He smiled. "Perhaps no one. We'll still perform. But I think there may well be an audience."

It hadn't occurred to the civic man that we might take possession of the theatre. So no one had cut off the lights or the telephone, though there was no heating because it was timed to go off from mid-day until two hours before performance time. Our doorkeeper could have fixed it, but when we gave him the option of siding with us he fled in a fury, and we locked the stagedoor behind him.

He spent a lot of time on the telephone getting his version of events out to the media. We sat huddled and hungry in the largest dressing-room, wrapped in bits and pieces from the company wardrobe. I managed to grab Von Rothbart's feathered cape from "Swan Lake". Someone else was wrapped in the Queen Mother's train. We looked like survivors from a fancy-dress party on a sinking ship. Finally he appeared, saying he expected us to give *everything we had* in this last performance. And there would be an audience, he said, he was pretty sure of that.

There was an audience. It broke its way through the police cordon and the bolted doors, seething with rage and excitement. The local media had taken up the matter immediately. Our sit-in and its motives furnished the main news item, and the idea of us gallant dancers shivering it out on a freezing February day to give a symbolic last performance of a banned work had caught the imagination of a wild and disparate set of people, from the artistic vanguard to the hooligans of the city.

Our administrator was to operate the houselights, the curtain, and the tape-recorder. (The stage lighting was computer-controlled.) He was white with fear – whether of his new responsibilities or their consequences, I don't know. We peered through peepholes from our side of the curtain and saw this violently merry mob taking over our pretty gold and crimson theatre. Climbing over seats, shouting from the dress circle, swigging from bottles – things I'd never seen a ballet audience do before or since. I felt that something of the "Sacre" pulse was already in them, dangerously awake. There had been the sound of breaking glass as they'd forced their way in, an exciting sound urging for more.

I felt a knot of worms shifting and contracting in my stomach, and had the idea – amazing insubordination – that we dancers should call it off, refuse to perform. But there was still that exploding carnival of energy out there to be appeased. We had no choice.

"Sacre" was the only work presented. You must dance it as a solemnisation, he said, as it was danced in antiquity, man's first groping towards a mystery. Remember, you are near-animals aspiring to be gods. Everything is possible. And remember also, that this is the last time.

We took our places, and waited. The signal was given. The curtain went up. There we were in the half dark, and the light creeping up to strength. The bleak pinched cadence of those six notes pierced the silence from somewhere out there. There was no humanising presence in the orchestra pit, no half-glimpses of bowing violins or flickering drumsticks. The music came out of nowhere, impersonal as thunder.

We stamped and beat, we swayed and flung ourselves in a pack. I danced without thinking, sucked back and flung out like spray, moved by the mass of our well-drilled, desperate bodies.

Then *he* came on with his strange loping ceremonial step, and made with each of us women a series of movements like a lover, like a buyer of flesh, like a soul-doctor. He went down the whole line like this, then turned, pausing at one, moving away, pausing at another. That was when I used to long for murder – a murder that would wipe out all the enchanted slavery of years of moving my limbs to the crack of his voice and the clap of his long hands.

Finally he stopped at Kati. But Kati that evening put up more than the usual struggle. She seemed to have grown roots, she wouldn't move. Finally, hissing, he swung her over his shoulder and carried her downstage, something not in the choreography. She should go, stumbling and falling, dragged by the arm.

Then started her long solo of agony. And at each attempt to escape, the circle of men penned her closer and tighter. This roused something like frenzy in the audience. They were leaving their seats, massing in the aisles. He made another change in the choreography, turning suddenly and threatening them. They moved back.

Kati danced in fear of her life, as the role should be danced. She was magnificent. I thought her bones would start through her skin in her desperation to escape – at all costs to escape. At last she fell on him, exhausted, sliding down his body to the ground, and they rushed forward, all the men, to drag her round by the hair, then to raise her up, hold her head down like an animal for the blade – then down came his hand in a great scimitar-slice on her neck and her body went limp.

A frightful shout went up from the audience. They started forward, crashing and clambering over the seats, yelling and screaming - baying, rather, it had the ring of hunting animals – and swarming towards the stage.

Too much happened too quickly. I saw his face, horribly exalted, just before they got to him. Then he was picked up bodily. Were they going to lynch him, or carry him round in triumph? At that moment the stage lights went dark and the screaming rose sharply. Then they came on again, as did the house lights. Once more everything went black, then bright again – what was going on? Someone grabbed my hand, and we fled backstage. We locked ourselves into a dressing room along with a dozen others, and waited in rigid terror, listening to the crash and breakage of that tidal wave of bison-power that the climax of our ballet had released. The last bars of the music were still sounding out.

And finally, we heard sirens, whistles, shouting of a different kind, and eventually, after a long time, a sickening quiet. When we crept out of our caves this time, the rite was over, and its victims lay on stretchers and were being carried out by firemen, police, ambulancemen. We were herded into the rehearsal room where a police officer called the company roll. All of us were there except Kati and him.

As her closest friend, I've had a hard time with the media. They've offered me a lot for an "inside story". I've tried to hold out – it seems so despicable to make money out of what happened to her – but now I'm desperate. Winter goes on and on – I sometimes believe we've killed spring with that monstrous performance. And I can't dance any more. All my joints have stiffened up.

There was, of course, a public enquiry. But long before that we knew that *he* had been rounded up inciting the mob to set fire to our beautiful Gothic town hall, and that Kati had died on stage. At first they thought she'd been trampled to death. Then it was revealed that her neck had been broken, result of a sharp blow such as a karate killer would use, and not easily explained by mob violence.

I go in absolute terror of hearing that music again. I now know that the rites can go badly wrong if the high priest is mad. And that is why certain tribes just die out and disappear – as our company has done.

Derek Ross

Stranraer

"It is difficult to be kind about Stranraer."
– The Rough Guide to Scotland, 1995

i: indignant

A suppose it's easy tae stick yer pen
in places ye ken nithin aboot. Tae
look doon fae lofty pages at grimy
High Streets, an never even try tae ken
a toon fae the inside. Ye'd hae tae spen
mair time than ye could spare tae delve intae
Stranraer's hidden hert. Still, ye're no tae blame,
toons are seldom as ye first perceive them.
Christ!, listen tae me defendin a place
a left before the ink on ma exam
grades wis dry. A'm a cliché, spoutin wurds
o indignation, tryin tae save face.
Jist like aa ma kind, wha'll no be back, an
wha left their accents on the straicht through bus.

ii: evening

The Sun bled,
poured its crimson
intae the depths
o Loch Ryan.
Orange-tipped clouds
congealed,
an fought tae staunch
the mortal wound.
An a stood
at the watter's edge,
an watched the life
drain fae the face
o the day.

Behin me,
the Clayhole glowed on,
indifferent tae
the fallin shroud.
A turned,
an loose stanes
rattled like aul banes.
A walked towards the lichts,

that wir
strung in a sneer
alang the al shore road.
The defiance warmed me,
as the al toon reached oot
an wrapped me in its erms.

Clayhole: One of the original villages which were amalgamated to form
the Royal Burgh of Stranraer in 1617 by King James VI and I. Has
become a nickname for the town.

v: origins.

A wid lean on the rail o the al pier,
cast stern een up the length o Loch Ryan,
an imagine square-sailed langboats ridin
the white horses. In a gulls' call A'd hear
a horn's blast, a battle cry, sense the fear
o the unbeatable. The origin
o Stranraer's name had tae be there, Vikin
fir "Safe Harbour", or sum such, had tae be.
But noo, years efter, a freen tells me that
the neme stems fae Gaelic roots. "Sron ramhair",
broad nose, the shape o Galloway. A knife
couldnae cut deeper, a'm no haein it!
A can still feel the wun lashin the pier,
yon wis nae sneeze, yon wis the breath o life!

Stranraer: There are, of course, alternative theories as to the origin of
the name. Prior to being made a Royal Burgh in 1617, the town gained
the rank of a Burgh of Barony in 1596. In this earlier charter the name
is written as Stranrawer. It is said by some that the name is derived from
the strand or rivulet that divided the 'raw' of houses on its banks.

Stake-Lines.

Stake-net fishing: An ancient and popular form of Salmon fishing on the
Solway Firth, in which nets are strung betwee⁻ lines of stakes, or poles,
which stretch out into the estuary.

i

This string of stakes
sticking out of Solway sand,
They are like the ribs
of some great Leviathan,
that, having spawned,
beached itself and died,
out of empathy, perhaps,

with the Salmon
that its skeleton
now traps.

ii

If I stand here
very still,
and use an auditory knife
to cleanse this carcass
of unwanted flesh,
I am left with
the harsh death-rattle
of the wind as it scrapes
past sinewed rope,
and the flip-flapping
of the seaweed
that clings
like dry, dead skin.

Waterloo Tower; New Abbey

To record the valour of those British, Belgian, and Prussian soldiers who under Wellington and Blucher on the 18th of June 1815 gained the victory of Waterloo by which French tyranny was overthrown and peace restored to the World. (*inscription*)

i

A sair climb it wis, clamberin up stane
steps slotted intae the hill like the teeth
o haaf buried skulls. We struggled tae keep
oor feet, an the trees drapped their stagnant rain
on unsuspectin heeds. Gaspin we gained
the upper grun, an fun the tower wreathed
in a cal April mist that crept an seeped
through sodden claes. Still, we were gled we'd came.
fir their wis somethin aboot yon tower,
mair o a folly than a monument.
Its inscription proclaimin a prood hour
o glory. But wis it pride that glowered
abin us, or wis it a sense o guilt
in the way young deaths are gloated ower?

ii

"The mair things change, the mair things stay the same.",
We a thocht it, but naebody dared tae
say it. This wis nae place fir al clichés.
Besides, somethin wis missin fae the stane
o the tower, nae regiment o names
merched doon its side, a mindin o the day
rether than the deed. Memorials hae
their place though, this yin tae. We made fir hame,
but this time took the easier way, doon
forest paths lined wi ranks o trees, straicht-backed,
formed up in perfect order, bein groomed
fir a bitter harvest. We stegged on, soon
reachin the New Abbey road. The sun dragged
itsel awake. Somewhar, a kirk bell boomed.

Mary Gibbons Illustration

The Chess Player

Head bowed, he dares
the board. His is
a cold arith-
metic. Life and

death, black and white,
war-game of the
mind. He commands
an army of

bloodless, faceless
soldiers. No cries
rise from wooden
throats, his castles

fly no battle
flag. The squares wait,
silent and clean,
for the combat

to begin. En-
grossed, we forget
the real World, where
real blood flows on

distant boards, and
fallen men can
not be boxed, then
resurrected.

Back here its just
another game.
We spectate and
pay homage to

our chess playing
God, who shifts and
snares a pawn by
its slender throat.

" As for Europe ..."
The fiction of Christine Brooke-Rose

Heather Reyes

Christine Brooke-Rose has the courage to be a European writer in the fullest sense, for her humour is decidedly British while her influences and enthusiasms have include French writers and theorists (Nathalie Sarraute, Alain Robbe-Grillet, Maurice Roche, Gerard Genette), as well as Beckett, Calvino, and that honorary European, Pound. Her reputation in Britain has suffered somewhat from her European orientation and our laziness in preferring less demanding texts.

In a *Guardian* article 1994 Booker Prize judge, James Wood lists *The Christine Brooke-Rose Omnibus*, containing four of her novels, *Out, Such, Between,* and *Thru* as one of "The Best Books Since 1945". He states his criteria to be books which are "deep and beautiful, which aerate the soul and abrase the conscience, and which have particular beauties of language and form – books which thus offer distinctly literary experiences, and yet which speak of the deepest human truths".

Born in Geneva in 1923 of a Swiss-American mother and partly Scottish father and educated both on the Continent and Britain, she grew up fluent in French and German as well as English. After serving in the WAAF during the war, she went to Oxford and then to London University where she gained her Doctorate in 1954. After several years spent writing fairly conventional novels and reviewing, she was excited by the novels of Beckett and by the new directions fiction and theory were taking in France and began to write in an entirely new way. *Out* (1964) won her the Society of Authors' Travelling Prize and considerable critical acclaim. Probably the least directly humorous of her books, this remarkable *mélange* of Beckett, Robbe-Grillet, science fiction, and cinema, reverses the 'normal' race/power relationship; black is not only beautiful, it is also healthy, privileged, and in control, the 'Colourless' having become weak and susceptible to disease and early death as a result of unspecified global catastrophes which have not affected the 'Coloureds'. We experience directly what it is like to be a poor and enfeebled white man in such a society, an outsider to our own, dominant power structures. The reader experiences all the sensations, conversations, actions and imaginings of the 'focalizing consciousness' of the sick white man, one time 'humanist' with a Ph.D., and now out-of-work odd-job man.

One reviewer suggested that "*Out* would make a fine *nouvelle vague* type of film", drawing attention to the highly visual quality of the writing and the cinematic technique of cutting from scene to scene, while also mentioning Brooke-Rose's concern with form and language and the influence of Beckett in the way that "certain phrases recur throughout the book, spiralling upwards and out, often with a shift of emphasis on the way" ('Boswell',*Scotsman,* 17 April 1965). Although each of her later novels is different, the combination established in *Out* of the highly visual with a sensitivity to language lies at the heart of their technique.

Her prize winning novel *Such* (1966) is, in many ways, less sombre and more expansive in which the discourses of jazz, astrophysics, and psychiatry are forced to speak to each other, suffused with Surrealist imagery. A psychiatrist is attached to a team of astrophysicists. After clinically dying and being brought back to life, Larry/Lazarus develops a different way of seeing the possiblilities for human life, saddened by the "banal untender story" of most relationship she wishes for a more meaningful existence that takes account of the real nature of Man's place in the cosmos. Larry's newly acquired 'radio-telescope' eyes see people in astrophysical terms – he sees their 'thingness'. And his voyage into inner space during his 'death' has given him an alternative family, each member representing an aspect of himself in his worldly life. His 'planet children' (slices of a hard-boiled egg removed from the knee of a 'girl-spy'– his replacement wife) are baptized with the names of Blues, after which they are flung away into space and return, one by one, at appropriate intervals during the text.

– ... I think we ought to get these baptised. You never know.

– ... Jonas will do it for us. We'll find him by the Travel Agent's swimming-pool.

We do. Jonas and his Jovials play primitive jazz on the opposite edge of the pool, which slopes down to the deep end, quite empty .....

– What shall we do without water?

– Stop fussing...Jonas does it with music.

He does. He places the first planet on the end of his trumpet, lifts the instrument to his big mauve lips and sobs out Gut Bucket Blues to the rhythmic counterpoint of clarinet, bass sax, trombone and drums. Gut Bucket moves off into his orbit. Jonas places the second planet on the end of his trumpet and plays Potato Head Blues, then, with the third, Tin Roof Blues, then Dippermouth Blues with the fourth and finally, to change the style, Really the Blues. Really follows his brothers into orbit. (pp.205-206)

Needless to say, a few lines can give little idea of the fun, pathos, and sheer ingenuity of a novel which the writer Elizabeth Smart described as a "Funny, painful, exciting, haunting book, one that is absolutely of our time in content and form" (*Queen,* 27 October 1966).

Between (1968) is the first of Brooke-Rose's novels to use a female 'focalizing consciousness'. She is a simultaneous interpreter who lives between languages and locations, both literally and metaphorically. Not only does she travel constantly between international conferences at which the world's problems are endlessly discussed, in her personal life she cannot 'be' anywhere – a condition acted out in the writing by the absence of all forms of the verb 'to be'. Legally divorced from her husband, she is waiting for an official annulment from the Catholic church. Although she no longer believes in the old world of male dominance and prescriptive religion, she wants an official recognition from it that she is free. In a collage of languages and discourses, we experience with her a life in which words alternately offer and block meaning. Past loves remembered and possible romances – or lack of them – in the future (her annulment finally arrives "just in time for the menopause") are woven into a succession of plane journeys and hotel rooms, all different, all the same, the label on the mineral water bottle being the surest indication of where you are. Façades of rhetoric, at conferences or in love letters, disguise the shabby realities behind them: in one humorous enactment of this, the 'big ideas' of "la verité, l'humanité, la justice" have "la tutungerie" tacked on the end. The text will be blocked for many readers, but once you know that "tutungerie" is Roumanian for tobacconist, the pathos of the phrase becomes a microcosm of what the whole text has to say in other ways about the 'grand narratives' of "this our masculine–dominated civilization".

It is in this novel that Brooke-Rose discovered what she could really do with language. The multi-lingual puns, repetitions, word-play, and sentences that change direction through 'hinge words' are never gratuitously employed: the opening up of meanings as words and languages fraternized "in a Misch-Masch of tender fornication" not only defines what happens in the text but suggests a model of enrichment through 'unclosed meanings' – relating to the wider, planetary context of the novel, for "We must love one another or die".

Thru (1975) is in many ways the odd one out among Brooke-Rose's novels. Typographically adventurous, it challenges the reader with cryptograms and patterned arrangements of the text, as well as with a narrative that continually cancels itself out. Exposing the 'fictionality of fiction', the novel deconstructs itself as it goes along bringings together Brooke-Rose's work as novelist and as literary critic/theorist. Brooke-Rose was aware that her most likely serious audience for such a work would be a handful of narratologists. She had been in Paris since 1968, had become absorbed in the new world of French theory and had perhaps not realised how little of it had travelled across *la Manche*. But despite the Continental bias of the text in some ways, it reveals a very British sense of humour, for although she 'uses theory', she also pokes fun at it and manages to avoid the deadly earnestness that often accompanies theoretical discourse.

The text of *Thru* results (on one level) from university creative writing classes, location unspecified and unimportant – but for those who wish it to be pinned down, Brooke-Rose has pointed out that the U.S.A could be the only likely candidate. (Creative Writing was not taught in French universities at the time and only at one in Britain.) *Thru* begins and ends with a pair of eyes looking at themselves in 'le rétroviseur' – the rear-view mirror – in itself an image offering a wealth of interpretations and recurring at various points during the novel.

> Through the driving-mirror four eyes stare back
> two of them in their proper place
> Now right on
> Q   ask us

to de   V   elop   foot on gas
how m(any   how)   eyes?

    four   two
       of them   correct

    on either side   of the
nose   the other

                              ▽
two   O danger
    slow   down
                              △
         eXact   repli-
cas

nearer the hairline further up the brow but dimmed as in a glass
tarnished by the close-cropped mat of hair they peer through

The mat of hair is khaki, growing a bit too low on the brow
the nose too big

Who speaks?

    le rétro   viseur   (some   languages
          more   visible than   others)   (p. 1)

unless the mirror is moved to the
                              sudden isolation
of seeing nothing whatever in the
                        rear
                 of
            the
       mind
    and
no
       narrator at all though this is only a
       manner of speaking since the text has
       somehow come into existence but with
       varying degrees of presence either bent
       or gazing into diasynchronic space or

          at the chain of phonic signifiers
          like Ali Nourennin the beardless
          Marx who takes no notes and stares
          with riveting eyes that break the chain
          assunder with a listening look

But it needs adjusting.

Sometimes the reader becomes involved in passages of more conventional narrative – only to have the security of this demolished by the interruption of a teacher's hand-written comment and grade, giving it the status of a mere 'exercise' and thus distancing us from it and making us aware of the processes of composition – and providing an additional source of humour.

The 'focalizing consciousness' of *Amalgamemnon* (1984) is that of a Classics lecturer about to be made redundant, her subject sacrificed to the advance of the technological sciences. She speculates about her future (the whole text is, appropriately, in the 'unrealized' tenses of the future and conditional) and necessarily about *our* future, for her situation as 'redundant' woman has universal implications. As with *Between*, an intensely personal and individual story is used to expose problems of global magnitude. In the long and lonely night ahead, the woman will choose to have her radio for company rather than the predictable snoring, self-satisfied lover, Willy. Snatches of different media discourses are heard – the news, weather forecasts, a D.J. announcing trivial competitions with trivial prizes, though they often come to us in a mutated form as the woman's mind plays with them, blends them with other thoughts, and brings out a more expansive meaning: a recipe becomes a reflection on political rhetoric, and the weather forecast has sinister implications – though, once again, humour precludes any hint of sententiousness:

> Take a human hair, split it in four, whip it up with the whites of their eyes, rehandle thoroughly with fresh modifiers finely chopped and pour into a battered wish, bake in a moderate speech for twenty minutes. Temperatures will drop to the right of the country, with frowns and intermittent wails but smiling patches here and there in the home counties. To the left of the country the temperatures will rise quite high with threat of storms and localized gnashing of teeth. Towards the south-west... As for Europe, shall we ever make it, will it be green or red or black and blue? (p.74-75)

The danger for us all is that the 'voice of woman' – in this case the prophetic voice of a modern Cassandra – will be silenced through forced amalgamation to the male: "...poor Cassandra will be enslaved by all Amalgamemnons and die with them not out of love but of amalgamation to silence her for ever" (p.20). All she can do is to go on trying to make her voice heard. "Perhaps," she thinks, she should "walk dishevelled the battlements of Troy uttering prophecies from time to time unheeded" (p.7) – or simply "make up a story" in her head, "unheeded and unhinged" (p.12). But if the voice of the prophetess goes unheard and, as seems likely, "we'll all go on as if" (one of a number of recurring phrases), then the consequences for us all will be dire.

Set against the female, prophetic voice of Cassandra is the voice of traditional male history, for among the many discourses merged and juxtaposed are passages from Herodotus' *Histories*. Although 'Cassandra' elects the richness of such texts in preference to the banalities of the discourses around her, the quotations from Herodotus are used to comment ironically on events in the novel and to point out the origins of male domination. In comparison with his sober and one-dimensional use of language about the past, the inventive, open-ended, playful language of the woman offers hope through its very method of discovering and making new and multiple possibilities – a hopefulness that is set in counterpoint with the dire warnings carried by that prophetic voice.

> Cabinet sources will make no comment and I shall mimagree, how should I not? Mimecstasy and mimagreement will always go together, like sexcommunication. Wouldn't it be better to mimage myself an Abyssinian maid, striking two small hammers on the cords of her dulcimer and singing of Mount Abora? Or a Cambodean child? Or a New York street-sweeper...? ...Meanwhile by way of exercise the Abyssinian maid will sing when I'll be born my primitive memory will be indelibly imprinted with the whale paradise that will expel me onto the shore of an unpromising land about to be torn apart. And won't all promised lands of milk and honey and all pleasure domes become battlefields of distant voices prophesying war...
>
> ...Sandra my love ... he'll exclaim ... we'll celebrate when you'll be rid of the university, when thanks to me you will accept, and face, being only a woman.
>
> A polar low will sneak down to the coast depositing snow everywhere. Soon the ecopolitical system will crumble, and sado-experts will fly in from all over the world and poke into its smoking entrails and utter smooching agnostications and we'll all go on as if. (pp.14-15)

'Warnings' are present, too, in Brooke's Rose's next novel, *Xorandor* (1986). The method of using a single focalizing consciousness is here abandoned and the story is told by twin children, Zab and Jip (girl and boy) who accidentally discover an ancient rock with which they can communicate through their computer. The rock – whom they christen Xorandor (after the computer's 'both/and' function, as opposed to the 'either/ or', in itself carrying an important message about attitudes and ways of relating to the world) – lives off nuclear material and seems the answer to the world's nuclear waste problem. However, Xorandor has a number of offspring, one of which tires of the second-rate food of 'waste', develops a taste for the real thing, and plays havoc with the world's so-called defence systems: there is no way of telling which weapons have been ruined. With a number of different genres lurking in the background (science fiction, Enid Blyton style children's adventure, political thriller), Xorandor is also about the difficulties of (re-)constructing a narrative and the differences between male and female priorities and ways of telling: the children are now exiled to Germany and attempting to write their story onto disc. Zab's description of their first sight of Xorandor – "it was brownish rather than grey, as the other rocks were, but with odd patches of dull greyish blue that shone faintly in the sun. Faintly cos the weather was hot but cloudy, misty even, heavy and stormy" – is dismissed by her brother as "essay-stuff": she must replace it with a description by shape, rather than colour and 'atmosphere': "the stone was sort of flattened and almost perfectly round, with vague bumps, or irregularities, here and there." (pp.15-16). Later Jip accuses Zab of including details that are irrelevant to the main line of the narrative (p.75), while Zab notes that her brother "fights shy of emotions, or any kind of complexity other than scientific" (p.80). "Emotions ... just don't interest you. Except perhaps your own", she berates him (p.132), adding, a little later, "You never listen to anything personal, Jip" (p.152). As with the previous novels, the connection is made between the stories we tell (and how we tell them) and the way the world is organised, what power systems are in place and their effects on values, priorities, and the possible future of the planet.

The conventions of science fiction stories impose expectations that Xorandor originated on Mars – and the rock seems happy to go along with this version if this is what the humans want, and even to be sent back to Mars. But the other possibility is that Xorandor has earthly origins and that the rock's kin, who will (unknown to humans) remain behind, will have been instructed to continue the neutralization of weapons. The twins know that if this other possibility should be revealed through their own narrative on disk, such a hope will be at risk. The book ends with them deciding to destroy their narrative - the next day. We aren't told whether they do or do not – the two possibilities of the ending mirroring the alternative versions of Xorandor's own story.

But the novel's sequel, *Verbivore* (1990), confirms that Jip did, in fact, keep the floppy disk recording their story (p.62). The global problem tackled in this book is the vast amount of unnecessary communication via the airwaves – the dense web of 'noise' humans have created around their planet. Some of Xorandor's offspring, forced to absorb all human communication, retaliate by 'eating' airwaves. But this does not just effect the banal and unnecessary types of communication with which we flood our world: vital information for aircraft safety, for example, is also in jeopardy. The implications are that unless we make intelligent decisions about how we use our resources and technological capabilities, we will destroy them (or be destroyed by them?). Rather than deciding for ourselves to adopt a more reasonable way of life, we will be *forced* back to a different set of skills and ways of thinking and living.

Zab is now an Euro-MP and Jip a high-flying scientist who has brain-drained to the U.S.. They have a hunch that the condition of 'verbivore' is connected with Xorandor and try to put things right and make people see sense before it's too late. But the end of the novel is pessimistic. As Zab and Jip watch the ten o'clock news, 'total verbivore strikes': "Blank screen, black with millions of white dots, like a universe" (p.196). As in the previous novels, *Verbivore* combines global concern with matters of narrative and how the two relate.

Brooke-Rose's most recent novel to date is *Textermination* (1991), in which a vast array of fictional characters from many places and periods try to forestall the 'extermination' of their 'texts'. They travel to San Francisco to attend a 'Literary Convention' to pray for continued existence, their prayers addressed to the Implied Reader in whose minds they are re-created and without whom they cannot exist. It is a wonderful carnival of a novel, the characters freed from their original narratives though continuing to behave in appropriate ways. Humbert Humbert, from Nabokov's *Lolita,* seems to have designs on Henry James' Maisie of *What Maisie knew, Middlemarch*'s Dorothea Brooke has earnest conversations with Hardy's Jude Fawley, while Sir Lancelot and Emma Bovary manage some heavy petting during a sightseeing trip to Death Valley; a band of Muslims attempt to poison Rushdie's Gibreel Farishta in a famous San Francisco sea-food restaurant, and the proceedings of the convention are interrupted by the rowdy arrival of a stream of TV characters demanding attention and attempting to take over. Inevitably, there is an earthquake (this *is* San Francisco) but, out of the disaster-movie scenario a number of characters crawl home to continue their life for a little longer.

While the novel's theme might concern the threat to literary culture posed by a modern technological society and recent theories of interpretation, the great procession of literary personages it presents us with reminds us of how firmly these characters are lodged in our consciousness: encountering them is like meeting old friends. Very few readers will recognise *all* of the characters, but even this has a positive effect: we know these characters represent riches we have not yet discovered and we are reminded of the enormous wealth of literature engendered by human activity down the ages and this makes us more appreciative of our humanity and the literature it has produced. The effect of reading the novel is exactly that hoped for by the characters when they pray to the Implied Reader – you and me.

> [Pope Hadrain VII is speaking] Dear friends and fellow characters, you all know the importance we attach to the power of collective prayer in this our desperate struggle for survival. Some of us have more existence than others, at various times according to fashion. But even this is becoming extremely shadowy and precarious, for we are not read, and when we are read, we are read badly, we are not lived as we used to be, we are not identified with and fantasized, we are rapidly forgotten. Those of us who have the good fortune to be read by teachers, scholars and students are not read as we used to be read, but analysed as schemata, structures, functions within structures, logical and mathematical formulae, aporia, psychic movements, social significances and so forth. ... We must pray to Him, to Our Implied Reader, Our Super Reader, Our Ideal Reader ... Oremus ... In the name of the Reader, and of the Interpreter, and of His Imagination. Amen. I will go to the altar of god. To the Reader who giveth joy to my youth.
>
> Judge me, O Reader, and distinguish my cause from the nation that reads not; deliver me from the unjust and the ignorant man.
>
> ... The reader be with you. ...The Beginning of the Holy Gospel according to Stendhal. ...Julian Sorel steps up to the book and begins to read in French. (pp.26-28)

The characters we are presented with are far from schemata, functions, formulae: a full-blooded life is restored to them - love, lust, anger, moodiness, pretensions, and all manner of individual quirks.

> When at last they reach Death Valley, Lancelot and Emma Bovary are in a state of high because as yet unassuaged passion from their heavy petting behind the high-backed seat in front of them. They get out with the others,

still flushed with fantasy-fornicating, but he hands her down gallantly from the carriage, the large swelling in the scarlet side of his tight hose still slightly pushing out his tunic of blue and silver damask. (p.110)

But among the fun and games we find the serious point of it all: "...the fate of the world depends, has always depended, on our ability to tell and to listen to stories" (p.126), but "It's a goddam miracle that fiction still has the power to offend, and maybe change things, as it used to" (p.35). But, of course, it is rarely works that remain outside the canon that change things. The issue of who is and who isn't included in the canon is acted out humorously in the novel by the presence of Mira Enketei (the redundant classic lecturer of *Amalgamemmon*) at the Convention, acting as a surrogate for Brooke-Rose herself. Both *Xorander* and *Textermination* itself are attributed to Mira – but, unfortunately, she is barred from the canon.

Although there has been a great deal of dismantling of the old canon in recent years – or certainly much talk about it – in any age there will be a number of books or authors that are considered to be more worth reading than others. The important question is not whether or not there is a Canon, but 'who made it?' The old dead white males syndrome is gradually fading as long overdue status is given to women writers along with those from other cultures but using English as their medium of literary creation. But while we enthusiastically read new literature from Nigeria, India, or the West Indies, which has the attraction of the exotic or different, we seem to have a more problematic attitude to literature with a Continental European bias. Attitudes to Europeanness, as well as to women writers who dare to be as profoundly and meaningfully inventive as Brooke-Rose, seem to have adversely affected her reception in Britain. It is an indictment of our narrowness that such a rich and innovative writer should be on university syllabuses in the U.S.A. but not always available in print on her own continent. One can only hope that the recent publication of her autobiography *Remake* (Carcanet) will continue the process of re-awakening interest in her work indicated by the two excellent volumes on her that appeared recently (Birch, Sarah. *Christine Brooke-Rose and Contemporary Fiction*. Oxford: Clarendon Press; Friedman, Ellen/ Martin, Richard (eds.) *Utterly Other Discourse*. Dalkey Archive Press.) While it is true that some kinds of literary and theoretical knowledge may enhance a reading of Brooke-Rose – as is the case with many writers – it is time that we foregrounded the humour, energy, compassion, vision and sheer fun of her remarkable novels.

Brent Hodgson

A Rant Agaynst the Sclater

Geten oute of my hous sclater.
Geten back to the occeane whair ye belang.
Stop rynnyng cross my carpet sclater,
And wes it you who eited upp my biskit?
That wes the dug? Sorry sclater.
Sclater, ye sholde be bigger,
So that whenne I jump on ye,
Ye geye SQUATT, ye littll monstour.

Hech me! Here cums anither yin ...

I Wes Lukand for the Yong Ladye

I wend out waukand, I hoiped to se hir.
Hir braid hippes, hir nek fyne and moir besydes.
The hieast trees, the settand sonne I dyde
Nocht gaup apon. I waukit throw hait aere,
Citie streits, the besy pepill amang.
Na sicht of hir, na sent of hir. I wald
Smell hir feit, kys hir taes I wald. Kys hir
Taes and moir besydes. Nou the derk hes cum,
I sched sum teirs an gife a sich. I lat
Fre my thochts a quhill: pennyfull the mune
Abufe the wattir, the wattir whilk dois
Glete and cule the nicht sa calme. The lume
Of daw is nocht neir. Togidder we coud ly
Doun and to hir I coud say – My Yong
Ladye, my Derrest One, may I luk apon
Your delicat feit? "Yes my lufe, bot fyrst
My blew sannies you hafe to whulp away ..."

3 a.m.

It hed to happen I suppois.
We thoucht the day wald cum.

Thare wer a few sterrs abowt yon nicht,
And O! the licht of the mune wes strang.

It wis clois 3am. The windo wes oppin.
The stretes of the citie wer silent,
And evin in the cot of the schepe hirder,
The man wes depe into a dreme.

Sumthyng flickered in the horizon.
It micht hafe bene a cowld sperk,
Or a swarm of thame: regardles,
It wes farr off. I wes wouk.
A sang on the rufe hed walknit me.

The raynne began to fall att 3 am,
Thane, the Universe cam to an end.

Foure Astronautis on the Planeit Darien

Frome quhair cummis the sound of the crunand?
The tone of that auld sang I thenk I knaw.
The paill grene licht of glofpming is lemand,
And throw the rochis I heir the blak wynd blaw.

Frome quhair cummis the speik of symmer?
The symmer-sessoun for the sikkir I mynde.
Abune the bray the goldin sterris glymmer.
I se craikand monstouris in the rochis clymbe.

Frome quhair cummis the sichand for hame?
Frome astronautis quha ouir the plane rile,
Frome thrie reskeweris quha to my beill came:
Petir Ros, Harie, Waltir of Argile.

THRIE POÉMES
Ingenrit from Owld Yrische Poetrie
Be
Schir Brent Hodgson
Of the Toune of Air

The Merle: The merle quho singis frome the wicir,
Hende his beik with nottis synceir;
The yallow beik of the onsair lowne,
Ay quhissillis a wyrit, plesand tone.

The Beis: To vissy flouris in feild and plane,
Befoir symmer be wynter is slane
The yallow beis frome flour to flour skipp.
Thay fle in the sonne withouttin rest
To vissy flouris thay lufe the best:
Gude is the gadderand in thair skepp.

The Merle: Singand merle, for you it is weill,
Sumquhar in the wuid is your beill.
Blak bewtie, na skellat you clang;
Sweit, saft, singular is your sang.

Parallelogram

Christine MacIver

Part One: Stupid

Sean and Shaun were born on the same day at the same time in the same ward of the same hospital.

Sean's father shot himself in the head four months after Sean was conceived, because he was conceived.

Shaun's dad planted a four month old tree four months after Shaun was conceived, because he was conceived.

When Sean was a year old, his mother shacked-up with another man. He told Sean, "You're stupid, just like your father, who shot himself." Sean stopped using his vocal chords.

When Shaun was a year old, he contracted meningitis. He made a full recovery, except that he was left completely deaf. His mum and dad learnt to sign, and they said to him, "I love you".

When Sean was three, his mother gave birth to a little girl, and named her Karen. Her dad doted on her. She was a beautiful baby. She was everything Sean wasn't; lively, noisy, happy and loved.

When Shaun was three, his mum gave birth to a little girl and named her Caron. Her dad doted on her. She was a beautiful baby, and just like Shaun, she was lively, noisy, happy and loved.

When Sean was four, his step-father was arrested. He and four other men carried out an armed-robbery on a bank. It went wrong. One of the gunmen was shot, and a customer was shot dead. The four other men were convicted of the crime and sentenced to eight years in prison. Sean's step-father was also found guilty of various drug-related offences and had his sentence increased by four years. When he went to prison, Karen screamed and howled; Sean said nothing.

When Shaun was four, his dad was killed. He worked in a bookshop as the assistant manager. He loved his job, and was good at it. Everyday, in the afternoon, he would pop into the bank next door to put some of the day's takings into the bank account, and get some change if any was needed. One day he went in during an armed-robbery. He was shot. Shaun's mum went mad for a bit; she was really erratic all the time. Shaun and Caron screamed and bawled.

Sean had to visit his step-father every week. He hated it because all his step-father ever said to him was, "Are you talking yet? No? I always said you were stupid." He didn't speak like that to Karen. He always made something for her, like a card or something out of wood. Sean would sometimes break Karen's present. He knew he shouldn't because it upset her, and he didn't like to do that. Karen was his only ally. It was just he was so angry and so jealous. But once Karen got upset, his mother got upset, and somehow she got around to blaming him for his step-father being banged-up. Although they both knew it had nothing to do with Sean, he never argued back.

Shaun had to visit his dad's grave every week. He hated it because the first few times he went there he thought he would see his dad. Instead it was just a stone and some grass. He knew his dad was never coming back, but he didn't know where he'd gone. Going to the grave meant his mum would cry, and then she would cry for the rest of the day. She would also get really moody, and Shaun would get blamed for things he hadn't done. His mum would go mad at Caron if she spilt food or made any sort of mess. Shaun thought this was unfair, but didn't think he should argue about it with his mum.

When Sean and Shaun were five, they started school. They were in the same class of the same school. The teacher thought it would be a good idea if they sat together, since they had the same name.

Sean's mother had said to the teacher, "He can't speak, but he's a smart boy." She had no idea how smart he was.

Shaun's mother had said to the teacher, "He can't hear, but he's a bright boy." The teacher was asked by the headmistress to learn sign language, and she taught the class, so it worked out well for everyone.

Sean hated Shaun. It was hatred that stemmed from jealousy, and was therefore a protective measure. He was jealous that Shaun's shirts were ironed. He was jealous that Shaun smelled clean. He was jealous that Shaun was made into a celebrity because the class had to learn sign language. He was jealous that Shaun had twelve coloured pencils against his meagre four. He was jealous that Shaun was loved and had a home and not just a place where he stayed. Sean wished a thousand times every day, every minute of every day, that Shaun would disappear and he could take his place. Then he would have ironed shirts, he would be clean, he would be a celebrity, he would have twelve coloured pencils, he would be loved and have a home. Sean only looked at Shaun when he wasn't watching, and he never said anything.

Shaun hated Sean. It was hatred stemming from fear, and was therefore a protective measure. He was scared of Sean because his fingernails were dirty. He was scared because Sean's hair was untidy. He was scared because Sean smelled. He was scared because Sean never looked at him, ever. He was scared because he didn't understand Sean. He was scared because of the thought Sean might hit him. He wanted to make friends with Sean for two reasons: nobody else was making friends with him, so he felt sorry for him; and he thought it would be safer to be Sean's friend than his enemy. Sean wasn't interested in being his friend. Whenever Shaun tried to communicate, Sean turned his back. After a while, Shaun gave up and concentrated on his work and being friends with the other boys.

Much to the surprise of the teacher and his mother, Sean was a smart boy. He worked hard, he worked well and he worked fast. He was always the first finished, with few or no mistakes. He never did his homework, however. Letters were sent to his mother, who said, "Do your homework, you stupid boy." He refused. She would make him get his book and his jotter out, and she stood over him while he sat doing nothing. She could have stood holding a loaded gun to his head, and it would have made no difference. The teacher found a way around this. She got Sean to do his homework during class. Because he worked so fast, he always had enough time. She would often give him other work too, because otherwise he would just sit at his desk doing nothing while the other children played. The educational psychologist decided that Sean was autistic. Little is known about autism, so Sean was sent to a speech therapist. The speech therapist was really good. He patiently went through a thousand sounds with Sean, while Sean sat staring at the wall saying nothing.

The teacher and Shaun's mum were pleased to discover how smart Shaun was. He was a slow diligent worker, but he made no mistakes. He was careful to do well, because this made his mother proud of him, and therefore made her feel good about something. If she felt good about something, she was more content, and if she was more content, then she was less erratic and more patient with Caron. Shaun mixed well with the other children, despite being deaf. They accepted him without question because he was lively and had a good sense of humour, and they picked up sign-language easily. Once a week he visited a speech therapist who helped him to talk. He found this difficult, but the speech therapist was patient, and Shaun came on in leaps and bounds. His lip-reading also improved, which made his life a lot easier. He was regularly assessed by the educational psychologist, who saw that he was adjusting well and settling into school-work and play.

Sean and Shaun did not sit together in primary two or three. They regarded each other across the classroom, without ever making eye-contact, and it would be fair to say that Shaun was the only person in the school with whom Sean had a relationship to speak of. Primary four was the first year the members of the class were allowed to choose beside whom they sat. Without any form of communication whatsoever, Sean and Shaun sat together in primary four, for the rest of primary school, and on into secondary school.

When Sean was eight, his mother visited a fortune teller. The fortune teller was around 45, with thick make-up and a bad sense of dress. She read Sean's mother's palm, and read her Tarot Cards. She was very accurate indeed: "You have a son, and a daughter. Your son is difficult. The man in your life has gone away, against his will. To prison, yes? Oh dear. He is a bad man. I see nothing of his future. That is not to say he has no future, just that I don't see it. Your daughter, she is beautiful, yes? She has been blessed with a generous and kind spirit. The gods have been good to her. Your son ... oh dear. No." She stopped. "Go on, go on," Sean's mother implored. "Suicide," the fortune teller sighed. "He is cursed." She frowned and shook her head. "I'm sorry, I have said too much. You watch him when he's sixteen" There was a long pause. The fortune teller sat with her eyes closed. Sean's mother was confused. "Is that it?" The fortune teller nodded. "I paid thirty quid for this rubbish!" Sean's mother shouted as she stormed out. The fortune teller called after her, "It's not rubbish." Sean's mother was dismayed that she'd only heard about Sean's step-father, Sean and Karen. There had been nothing about her. She thought about the suicide thing. Sean's step-father was due out of prison the year Sean would be sixteen. It might be better for everyone if ... She pushed the thought to the back of her mind.

When Shaun was eight, his mum met Jesus. She was sitting on a bench in the cemetery where her husband was buried. She wasn't crying or anything, just sitting. An older woman came and sat beside her. For a while the woman just sat too, then she spoke: "Hello." Shaun's mum looked up. She hadn't noticed the woman. The woman continued: "Have you lost some-body?" "Yes, my husband." "Oh, I'm sorry. My son died. A year ago today. He was 12. Killed by a drunk driver. I never got a chance to say 'Good-bye'." "My husband was shot in a failed armed-robbery one day when he was putting money in the bank. I never got to say 'Good-bye' either. I keep thinking he'll come back. But nobody ever comes back." "Jesus came back." "What?" "From the dead." Shaun's mum was horrified. She thought this line of conversation was a bit sick. But the woman went on, "Do you know Jesus?" "Jesus Christ?" "Yes." "No. Well, only from Sunday School, and that was a long time ago. I don't really want to know him." "Why not?" "I blame God for my husband's death." "Did God shoot your husband?" "No, one of the armed robbers did." "Then blame the armed robber." "It's not just that." "Then what?" "For many weeks before his death, he talked about one of his work colleagues who was a Christian. They had long discussions about Christianity, which left my husband troubled. The night before he died, he came home from work so excited. He said that during his lunch hour he'd prayed with this colleague and become a Christian." "Where do you believe your husband is now?" "In Heaven." "Why?" "Because he made peace with God before he died." "And don't you want to be with your hus-band when you die?" So Shaun's mum became a Christian.

When Sean was twelve, he started to listen to popular music. He never listened to the radio or watched the television in his house. Instead he would sit by himself in his room and read a book or draw. One day, in school, he passed the janitor's room, and heard Queen's *Bohemian Rhap-sody*. He had never heard anything like it in his life, and was very excited by it, so he knocked on the door. Since there was no reply, he went in, and saw the room had no-one in it, so he had a look around. On the desk sat a battery powered radio, from which the music was coming. Sean took it, and rewarded himself by taking the rest of the day off school and spending it in his special hiding place in the park. He listened to the radio there until dusk, then he went back to his house, where his mother was waiting to tell him he was a "stupid boy for staying out so late," and that she was "worried sick" about him. He went straight to his room and sat listening to the radio until the batteries went flat. After his mother had gone to bed, Sean went down to the sitting-room where his mother's stereo sat. He looked at it and contemplated. Nobody ever used it because the TV was always on. His mother only listened to the radio in the kitchen when she was washing-up. He took the stereo up to his room and listened to it all night. In the morning, Sean went back to school as normal, except that before the bell went in the morning, he put the radio back where he had found it. Every night after school from then on, Sean listened to the radio until he fell asleep. At first he listened to anything, but he became more selective as he got to know the music better. He liked the rocky stuff best, especially Guns n' Roses. One day he went into the local record shop and stole the Guns n' Roses *Appetite for Destruction* album and listened to it and the radio on alternate nights.

When Shaun was twelve, he became a Christian. After his mum became a Christian, he was taken to Sunday School every week, and to bible club on Wednesdays. At first he hated it because there was lots of singing, which he couldn't hear or understand. His mum had to go to Sunday

School with him to sign for him, but after a few months, various members of the congregation came forward to say they had been called to a signing ministry, and could they help out with Shaun. Shaun wasn't too chuffed initially, because he liked his mum doing it, but she didn't want to miss the sermon every week, so Shaun agreed to have these strangers sign to him. Soon he got used to the people (they took turns in accompanying him to Sunday School) and he discovered he liked them. They were all patient with him, and caring. Some of them even made him laugh. One of the signers was an eighteen year old boy who took Shaun under his wing. The two of them became quite close, and the older boy told Shaun a lot about Jesus. Shaun liked this boy very much, because he was the first proper male role-model Shaun had had since his dad died. Shaun's mum and the eighteen year old (who was a twenty-two year old by the time Shaun was twelve) both said the relationship was good, and that that was what Church was all about. You can be friends with people of all ages, and teach them, and learn from them, and have fellowship. Shaun liked this. He asked the now young man, "Why are you so good to me?" The young man answered, "I'm trying to be like Jesus. The Holy Spirit helps me." Shaun said, "I want to be like you. I want to be like Jesus and be helped by the Holy Spirit." The two of them prayed together, and Shaun, like his mum and dad before him, became a Christian, and proclaimed Jesus as Lord. (Hallelujah!)

When Sean was fourteen, he started to use his vocal chords again. He worked for a local newsagent as a paper boy. With the money he earned, he bought the albums of all his favourite bands. He also bought a personal stereo, and batteries to power it. He listened to the personal stereo while he was doing the paper round, and while he was walking to and from school, and almost all the time, but he still listened to the radio on alternate nights to hear new music. It was on the radio one evening he first heard the Nirvana anthem *Smells Like Teen Spirit*. As soon as he got his wages, he bought the album *Nevermind* and listened to it constantly. Within a few weeks, he knew it word for word. That's when he took a day off school and went to his special hiding place in the park with his personal stereo and *Nevermind*. He started by nodding his head in time with the music, but by the end of the first side he was humming along, by the middle of the second side he was singing the choruses, and he joined in all of the last song, *Something in the Way*. He listened to the album again and again, singing every word, until the time school ended, when he went back to his house. Although he was very excited, he said nothing to his mother, because he didn't trust her to react well to hearing his voice. Instead, he waited till the next day at school.

When Shaun was fourteen, he heard his mum talking for the first time since he was one. Shaun had left Sunday School, and was allowed to stay for the whole service. He liked the evening services because they were more informal. The church's minister preached most of the time, but sometimes a guest speaker was invited. One evening an African man came to preach. He said, "Jesus did not heal people to give them faith, but healed them because of the faith they already had." He said, "In Africa everyone expects to see miracles, and because they have that faith, they see the miracles, but here there are no miracles because no-one expects them. The people in this country have no faith." At the end of the service,

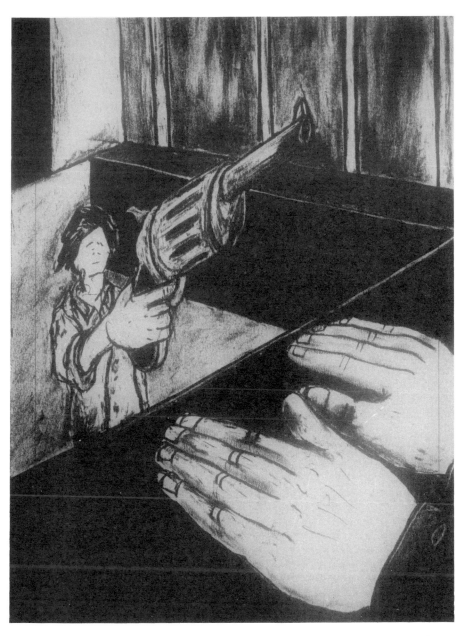

Alistair Niven's illustration

Shaun went up to the African man and said, "Will you pray for me?" Shaun, the African man and the minister went into the vestry and prayed for God's healing power to come on Shaun. And it did. Shaun was so excited, he rushed to tell his mum, and they cried together, and thanked God.

Sean and Shaun sat together in their first period class, which was Maths. In the middle of the lesson, while the teacher was explaining how to work out a particular problem, Sean sang softly, "I'm so happy 'cause today I found my voice, it's in my mouth." Shaun said, "I hear you."

Part II: Stupider

When Sean and Shaun were sixteen, on 5 April 1994, three things happened: Sean's step-father got out of prison, Shaun's mum remarried, and Kurt Cobain, Nirvana's angst-ridden singer shot himself in the head. Sean was distraught on two counts, and Shaun on one.

The first thing Sean's step-father said to Sean was, "Did you hear about that stupid singer? He did the same thing as your old man. What a stupid thing to do. I don't suppose you've got anything to say about that. You're too stupid to speak."

Sean ran away from home. He didn't know where he would go, or what he would do, but he was never going back.

Meanwhile, Shaun was watching his mum tell some man she would remain faithful to him and love and obey him 'til death did them part. He and Caron had had their mum all to themselves for years, and he did not want this man coming and taking her away from them. He also ran away. He did not know where he was going or what he would do, and he did not intend to stay away forever, he just wanted to give them a fright.

Sean had a plan of action. He knew there was a gunsmith on the high street, and he decided he would go there. Once inside the shop, he did not know exactly how he would get a gun, but he was determined. He looked around for ages, and the shopkeeper seemed unconcerned. After a while, Sean struck up conversation with the man. He bluffed his way through quoting lines from *Terminator* and *Terminator 2: Judgement Day*, and eventually he persuaded the shopkeeper to show him some guns, and just like in *Terminator*, he loaded the gun and held it up to the man's head.

The man said, "You can't do that."

Sean replied, "I can do whatever I want."

Unlike Arnie, he did not shoot the man. He left the shop, gun in hand.

Meanwhile, Shaun escaped the wedding reception, and ran to the park. He was just wandering aimlessly, wondering if they had noticed he was missing yet, and wondering where they would look first. He supposed he should have told his mum how he felt, but he was too scared. He thought she might have told him to sling his hook. He didn't have a clue where to find a place to live, or where he would get the money to live on if his mum didn't want him anymore.

Shaun continued to wander, absorbed in thoughts of rejection, and as he wasn't keeping a close eye on where he was going, he almost literally fell over Sean. They stared at each other incredulously for what was only a few seconds, but felt like years. Sean was pointing the gun to his head.

Shaun spoke first: "What the hell are you doing?"

"I'm stupid," Sean answered, looking away.

"Give me the gun," Shaun said. No response.

More emphatically, "Give me the gun!" Still no response.

"GIVE ME THE FUCKING GUN!" Sean looked at Shaun, almost shocked.

"You don't swear," he said.

"You don't talk," Shaun replied. They looked at each other for almost a whole minute, until Sean put the gun down. He grinned, then frowned.

"My step-father is out of jail, Kurt Cobain is dead, but I am sixteen, and I don't need to live at home anymore. I could get my own place, I could get a job, I can do whatever I like."

"You're not going to shoot yourself, are you?" They could both hear the panic in Shaun's voice.

"I'll live in the yard, I'll keep myself hard, I'll keep myself homeless and heartless and hard. I'll sleep under stairs along with the heirs of nothing and nothing means no-one who cares," Sean said.

"But Jesus loves you dear, and he's loved you hundreds and thousands of years," Shaun replied.

"You know that song by Belly?" Sean couldn't believe it.

"Yes. It's not exclusive to you. Come on, let's go."

"Where?"

"To the police. We'll hand in the gun."

"We can't."

"Why not?"

"I'll get done for theft and being in possession of a fire arm, or something."

"I'll say I found it." Reluctantly, Sean gave in. He handed the gun to Shaun, who hid it inside his jacket, and they headed towards the police station.

"How do you know Jesus loves me?" Sean asked, suddenly.

"It says in the Bible that Jesus came to earth to save those who are lost because he loves us. He died for you like he died for me, and he loves you like he loves me," Shaun told him.

There was a long pause, then Sean said, "Kurt Cobain was my hero."

"Some hero."

"I know. He shot himself. My dad shot himself, too."

"Is that where you got the idea?"

"Yes."

"Do you really want to be dead?"

Sean shrugged. After some time he asked, "Why are you here? I mean with me, going to the police?"

"I don't really know," Shaun replied. "I didn't want you to shoot yourself."

"You're OK, you know that? You can borrow any of my albums you want, anytime."

Shaun smiled. So did Sean.

Stuart A Paterson

from the 'MacSnail Poems'

MacSnail

They said that it cuid no be duin,
they mocked me, ilka two-faced wan.
The last lauch, though, maun go tae God
wha laboured lang on gastropods –
for ocht that fits intae a shell
will slide intae a plaid as weill.
And whusper it in Essex not,
but the Creatur is a Scot.

MacSnail Ponders Religion

As ower knowes and bens I crawl
and by the loch-sides bienly lurch,
I fash my insular, eternal saul's
still ower fast and furrit oweraa
tae be accepted by the Wee Free Church.
Though, at thon Final Judgement Bell,
will God tak *thaim* intae his shell?

A Famous Scottish Poet Encounters MacSnail

Graund chieftain o the gastropods
wha skites and sprachles ower the sod,
your creeshie corp I noo behaud
wi braithless prattle.
Fegs, he maun be a fu'some God
wha gars ye sprattle.

O aa the craturs He has made
baith wee and muckle, fell and snade,
frae flittermoose tae horny-taed,
ye bear the gree
wee stibble-rig o gress and road
wha luiks at *me*.

I maun seem as a birk or aik
heich owerheid ye as ye straik
through syle and clart, straucht on your braik
mayhap a god
wha'd gie ye sic a muckle glaik
gin ye daur faught.

As weill, then, that I jouk sae fast
across your wey, that I hae passed
afore your een hae hauf-wey grasped
the fact o me.
And noo I maun be less than vast
tae catch your ee.

MacSnail Galore!

The oft-accepted fact aboot the snail's
that slime maks up thon slippy-glintin trails . . .
                    but in Scotland . . .
MacSnail is different, foalla'd by his fauts
in snail-wide, 45%-proof mauts.

The Duke of Sutherland's Statue

Don't be deceived by grand looks or appearances,
don't trust in statues put up for the Clearances.
High on a pulpit of hill, like the steeple
of some ruthless kirk sneering down on the people,
its echoes of sermon still twisting the land . . .
a god-sized endeavour for one little man.
If there's a hereafter and justice at all,
then a million blunt chisels are sculpting his soul.

Night Noise

That sound outside, from over the bridge
and up the river, a high wild wailing
winding down to a low, long growl of echo,
has me up in my chair, neck hairs tight.
You'd tell me it's a heron out on the scope
for trout, or else a dog losing the head
to the vast, dark freedoms of its night.
Part of me wishes you here with your words
of brush-off logic, impatient dismissals
of thoughts on bogles, brownies, shades,
you who are out there too, unaccounted for.

Yet, part of me thrills (the part still
too unsure to rise and draw the curtains),
like a vole forced into the bright desperation
of winter moonlight on snow, seeking proof

of something other than it on the go,
trembling and held somewhere between
warm safety, hunger, and the old need-to-know.

Ann MacKinnon

Tara

Upon the hill at Tara monstrous stones
Shield the ashes of a dead kingdom
The Celtic symbols protect powdered bones
Of a people out of their time in wisdom.
These burial stones were dragged weary miles
Across country to be carved with care
By hand and flint into intricate styles
That we might visit and worship there.

Yet, not for us, this long-term remembrance.
For we are used to unencumbered death.
At the end we are but an audience.
Our dead slip easily away and we stand
Wishing we had carried their burial stone
And laid them back in their natal land.

Callanish

Silvered and smooth-grained
By generations of hands
Touching a talisman
The stones remain

While unspoken prayers echo
As the Wind-God shrieks
His despair for this bereft place.

Only pilgrims worship here
And urge these dolmens
To yield up their silence.

January, 1996

In this dark January
death thrusts at me
as dead whales rot on the sand
and birds call over them.

A poet answers cryptically
but his images define, as he lights
a cigarette and allows one last poem
to trail down the page.

The country toasts the bard
who brought us love
in a red, red rose
and taught us tolerance.

A friend dies alone,
his imagination curbed,
but his creations remain,
a celebration of a mind so full

That he could no longer
control it and let it engulf him.
He courted death and left the
future to us.

A cairn is built for hundreds
who died but we can only mourn
a few special people
this dark January.

Hebridean Funeral

Black-clad, they trudge
behind the plain pine box.
Heads bent, eyes lowered,
following him to the grave.

The sea beats on this
desolate shore and seagulls
cry for more, for more
above the wave's roar.

Another age beckons, but
they cling to custom
and carry him to the
headland of his birth.

No tears or words, stiff
faces, carved from bleakness,
as they lower the box
inch by inch into darkness.

The wind sears them
as they return the body
to its home and the earth
pulls him back to her womb.

We Were: A True Story

Gael Turnbull

We were a select company, almost two dozen, on a morning of unspectacular drizzle, toward the unravelling end of a year perhaps best forgotten. The building, states an architectural guide, is of reconstructed granite, in a subdued cinema style with a decorous jazz modern decor. Even within, we were glad of our overcoats.

Someone signalled to us to stand, as four men entered carrying on their shoulders a man-sized slightly tapered oblong box with brass handles. This was placed on a sort of dais with poles at the corners. What appeared to be a large grey blanket was then draped over, so that the effect was of a cut down four poster bed completely hiding what was beneath.

After we sat down again, two men read narratives from a lectern. One was carefully factual, with a scattering of opinion, on and about the dead man. The other was fictional and composed by the dead man, although of course while still alive, carefully shaped and well observed, with occasional amusing ironies. I can't remember if we laughed and perhaps not. Both narratives were concise, both apt to their purpose.

An official then entered and beckoned that the occasion was over and we filtered out slowly, shaking hands at the door with the brother of the dead man. Three of us exchanged greetings nearby and agreed that something more was appropriate, even necessary, perhaps just refreshment. But where we might find it became a problem.

The first two places we tried were not open. Then a coffee bar was, although there were only two stools at a counter and the three of us. Nonetheless, we ordered coffee. At which point, one of us discovered she had no money; another only enough for one cup. The third, luckily, was able to make up the difference. We talked, inevitably, of the dead man who had composed the fictions, and inevitably of our regrets that we had not seen him as much or as recently as we now wished. There were even regrets that we had not done certain things we might have done, and so on. At the same time, we reassured each other that what he had written would survive him, even probably, us. That it would become part of the sum of what has enriched the world, at least in our own country, and that it was not all in vain.

But one of us was not well, another had pressing things to do, and the third, perhaps rather numbed by it all, was struggling to make conversation. So we parted, on our several ways.

As for that oblong box with brass handles, last seen disappearing under that grey pall, we had no knowledge. Perhaps it is still there. Perhaps it was empty, or contained only ballast. Perhaps the same box is used for all such occasions. Perhaps the man who composed the words and because of whom we were there would have approved of such avoidance of waste.

Certainly what might or might not have been in that box and what might have become of it, has a very curious connection with the man who composed the fictions, for there is a connection. As there is between these words and the occasion described, between fiction, to whatever extent it is a fiction, and what is called reality, which may appear to exceed fiction. And if his stories were based on life, so this one is based on his life's ending, for all stories must end, and especially true ones.

New Scottish Writers

A Conspiracy of Hope, Michael Cannon, Serpent's Tail, £9.99; *The Year's Midnight*, Alex Benzie, Penguin, £7.99; *Quite Ugly One Morning*, Christopher Brookmyre, Little Brown, £12.99.

Three novels by three up and coming Scottish writers. And all three published by English presses. I don't know whether to be pleased that Scottish authors who are recognized as Scottish and not British are finding a wider audience with these presses or to be slightly depressed that, once again, Scottish publishers are losing out good writers to the big conglomerates down south. Either way I am impressed by the range that these new writers express in their writing. They take the familiar genres of the thriller, the coming of age novel and the historical novel and work them in a new and, can I say, Scottish style.

A Conspiracy of Hope, Cannon's second, is a difficult novel to pin down in a few paragraphs. It is split in two halves, the first being about the two main characters' early sexual awakenings and how their lives change after their experiences. Mainly, it's about the search for sex, how much fun it is, the trouble it causes. Examining each gender Cannon shows how men and women relate, or don't, when it comes to first sexual experiences.

His main character Jamie is a true manipulator, both cocky and lazy. He does everything he can to avoid work and to get what he wants from the people around him, specifically sex. But you can't help but like him. He is that boy in school you always envied; the one who spoke back to the headmaster, always got by on his wit and sharp tongue. You wish you were more like him no matter how much you basically loathed what he got away with.

The other character, Rachel, is less well defined and considered. Early on her motivations are quite clear; to get away from her parents and to experience sex. After they are accomplished she seems to become more of a plot device in the author's attempt to make Jamie grow up. She just becomes a blur.

The last half of the novel seems to have no firm foundation. The characters are older but no wiser. They tiptoe around each other and their lives trying to come together, but as the first half points out, neither have any idea of commitment or how to have an adult, stable relationship. They attain a bit more depth in this half, but by then it's easy to lose interest. I found the first bit on Jamie good enough to stand as a short piece on it's own, but after that the novel progressively loses coherence.

Michael Cannon seems to be struggling on too many levels here. He starts off with an upbeat, witty Scottish novel full of sex, middle-class versus working-class humour, but he suddenly turns to an in-depth study of dysfunctional relationships and the characters' psychological manoeuvring. Separately they would work well, but in trying to stick the two together he loses control and his readers.

Alex Benzie's first novel *The Year's Midnight*, on the other hand, is impressive and coherent. It is well-written and thought out. Benzie has a good feel for his characters and setting, the Aberdeenshire countryside during the early twentieth century. His use of dialect lends its hand to this charming story, although it is thick and often exhausting to get through.

The story of 'Watchie' Leckie, an apprentice watchmaker, and the problems his choice of employment cause is not terribly original. There are few unexpected twists in the plot, but Benzie has a solid control over the story and works it well. Watchie struggles to gain permission and acceptance to learn the art of watchmaking and eventually is asked by the town to fix a local clocktower destroyed by the townspeople a century before. Through all this he has to fight the prejudice of his father who believes he should be a farmer like generations before him and the strength of his obsession which almost threatens to kill him. There is also the side plot of his love for a young lower class girl which is thrown into conflict with his obsession for his work and a too eager local troublemaker. These elements combine well, but the novel slows down a bit with this second plot complication.

The only problem I have with this novel is the length and the attention to detail. The press release says that the novel started out as nearly 900 pages long. Shortened to around 600 it is still too much. Benzie gives you huge amounts of information on everyone and everything about this tiny village. We follow the Leckie family through two generations before we get to the meat of the story. And the development of Watchie as a clockmaker is delved into with excruciating detail. Benzie uses reams of paper to describe characters when one distinguishing attribute would do. One example I found that stood out in my mind was the village Provost. We are given a long account of his shoe business, his lust for success and his wife. What makes him an individual and interesting character however, is the fact that even though he has problems with his lungs if he exerts himself he still walks the long flight of stairs up to the clock tower to see Watchie's work progress. Several times we watch him struggle up the stairs to watch his dream being fulfilled. A little detail like that goes a long way. Benzie does give his story a solid believable feel and once you get to the central plot you have gone through half the book, so the next 300 pages are a breeze.

Christopher Brookmyre's *Quite Ugly One Morning* is short, sharp and amazingly witty considering the subject matter. The thriller, which includes a conspiracy plot and a murder mystery, revolves around the horribly mutilated body of a doctor found in Jack Parlabane's building. Jack, a journalist, wakes up with a hangover and immediately finds himself wrapped up in the case. Unfortunate circumstances for most, but he jumps in and finds out more than anyone bargained for. He manages to use his journalistic and slightly more criminal skills to follow the clues into a twisting conspiracy within the NHS.

Though the story contains some violent and graphic scenes the novel is entertaining due to the sheer extremes that the characters go to and the ridiculous things that happen to them. The characters, even the minor ones, are believable and realistically funny. Set in Edinburgh, Brookmyre has a good feel for the capital's people and places (note the mention of *Chapman*'s local the Barony). But it's Brookmyre's wit that carries the novel beyond regular thrillers. He manages to keep a steady flow of smart remarks and subtle jokes going without losing the feel or the fast pace of a thriller. He pokes fun at the genre as well as writing within it exceedingly well. You could almost see this done as a film, the scenes are so well planned out. Brookmyre is one to watch out for.

Gerry Stewart

Red Riding Hoods!

D'Alembert's Principle, Andrew Crumley, Dedalus, £7.99; *Buck Falaya*, James Killgore, Polygon, £7.99; *House of Lies*, Colin Mackay, Black Ace Books, £14.95

D'Alembert's Principle is an uneasy as well as a compulsive read; it's one of those books that plays so many tricks on the reader that it's rather like having a practical joker in the house. One turns each page with a certain nervousness. Crumley, like the enigmatic beggar Pfitz in Part Three, is a fine storyteller, but no sooner does the reader become hooked than the plot is snatched away again. Characters die at the point when one becomes thoroughly involved in their fate, except that death, especially that of Magnus Ferguson (whoever 'they' are) has a lack of finality about it that becomes part of a bewildering mathematical proposition. But there is far more to get to grips with here than mere postmodern junketing. In Part One D'Alembert has a pathetic dignity, Justine a longing for intellectual understanding, and Julie a silent emptiness at the heart of her story, all of which involve the reader to the extent that, instead of simply feeling cheated of a story, one is convinced that it is the characters, as well as the reader, whom life has cheated. D'Alembert finds meaning in a rigid schemata that is clearly absurd, and yet his fear of ambiguity has made him a mathematical genius: "words were no more than tokens of exchange; numbers on the other hand had a value that was eternal and unalterable". The irony is that numbers, like words, turn out to be signs full of ambiguity. Since this reader would not usually turn to the theory of calculus either for moral comfort or intellectual excitement, the subsequent undermining of D'Alembert's principle reads to her more in the nature of a firework display than the deconstruction of a theorem, but the fireworks are beguiling, and the bewildering improbabilities that are illuminated leave one wondering all over again what can possibly be real. The Enlightenment Paris setting adds piquancy, and historicity, to this otherwise eternal question. However, the ending, in which every story, every character, every image, seemed to have been exploded into nothing, along with total abdication on the part of the narrator, has some of the bleakness of ashes on the morning after: "I personally cannot vouch for any of it, and must now bring my account to a close, so that those readers wishing further diversion must, I fear, seek it elsewhere".

Those seeking further diversion in Killgore's *Buck Falaya* will find something very different. A weak-stomached reader, who does not wish to know about ways of torturing small animals that he has not previously heard of, may have difficulty getting past the second page. I would strongly advise perseverance. This cheerless beginning has a point: the central theme of this novel about childhood is the evocation of danger. Violence is always close, savagery always just around the corner. The animal motif, which becomes centred on the pig Traveller, is as unsentimental as the portrayal of the two brothers and Tyler, the three children at the centre of the book. Adult violence lurks on the edges of awareness, and David's terror of the Billyjack in the old forest epitomises his fear of what lies just outside the boundaries of his known world. Early on, memory is established as a key that has been lost. David has no memory of his mother's violent death, Rankin's memory of his father tearing up letters after she dies has no meaning, and the explanation that comes to David as a young man is partial and uncertain. And yet both boys know all the time what is never articulated, and their behaviour bears this out. Rankin's knowledge leads him first to cruelty – and yet even the small creatures tortured to death are given decent burial – and then to obsessive care for Traveller. Traveller seems to represent a fragile healing process, as the pig himself is permanently under threat. One waits for his extinction, and indeed eventually it comes, but perhaps by that time Rankin is already safe. We never know: the book ends on this crucial question. David, the younger brother, who is also the narrator, is made vulnerable by fear. His fear of the rope swing makes him the victim. He is subject to Rankin's teasing, and yet in the end it is Rankin who is the victim of adult violence. His father wounds him with words, and would have beaten him again if Reives had not covered him with weals already.

It's very much a book of the American South. In both setting and in its portrayal of the cruel vulnerability of childhood, it took me back to *To Kill a Mockingbird* and perhaps even to Faulkner. It's a brave man who can write about children and pigs in the wake of recent box office successes, but this book belongs to a tradition devoid of sentimentality, and an astringent mind rises well above the possible connotations of the subject matter.

Colin Mackay's *House of Lies* is also astringent, but the narrative is surprisingly uneven. There is an occasional crudity in technique that one would not expect from the author of *The Song of the Forest*, and the hard-line leftism is depicted with more anger than subtlety: "There are people who do really do talk like that" (p. 46). Should one need this kind of assurance? Certainly the five bigots who inhabit the Red House are too close to caricature for either their motivations or their ghastly fates to trouble the reader unduly. Those who drown in the blood of their victims elicit most empathy, and the reader may well have the same feeling by the end of the book. Where the violent images in *Buck Falaya* are frighteningly implicit, here they are endlessly explicated.

However, there are redeeming features. Tam is a strong enough central character to sustain interest, and each time the narrative returns to him its life is renewed. The best scenes combine the realistic details of being a night watchman with the spookier manifestations of the supernatural. These leave one feeling that being a night watchman is a heroic occupation, as it involves guarding the city against the perpetual nightmare of the repressed masses that throng the guilt-ridden unconscious of the community. Tam's awareness of the mysteriously sealed fourth floor has psychic as well as political (as a simile of the Berlin Wall) connotations, that offer a welcomed ambiguity in interpretation. The draped VDU that appears for a moment as a caped figure is genuinely scary in a way that roomfuls of blood and Stalinist statues come to life simply are not. Tam, one feels, deserves to be more than a counter in an outdated game. One would like to know about his daughter before one was halfway through the book. He, and Charlie perhaps, have an inner life which is a stronger counter to absolutism than any amount of anger, or blood and fire.

Margaret Elphinstone

Shoot to Score

Collected Poems, Flora Garry, Gordon Wright Publishing, £7.95; *Case Histories & Other Poems*, Ellis Sopher, Taranis Books, £5.99; *Seeing the River,* Raymond Friel, Polygon, £6.95; *Balancing on a barbed wire fence,* Jack Withers, Argyll Publishing, £6.99;

It is essential that poetry has a sense of focus whether it be in time, space, ego, language or ideology. It is this very focusing that allows any poem to be universally understood, allows any reader to step from their world into the thoughts and pictures of the poet and feel and understand and empathise with what is written. The worst poetry is that which has no focus, that simply floats without reference leaving the reader unable to attach with the ink on the paper...

Flora Garry's *Collected Poems* is simply a beautiful book. Flora takes us to the rural Buchan and the world which she knew as a young woman. We step into this world and witness the astonishing beauty of her native land, the turning of the seasons, the folk who worked the farms, and in the distance the ever approaching horrors of the war in Europe. We see this world completely, hear its rhythms and changes clearly, through the language, both English and Scots, that Flora uses in her poetry.

In the brief space of 'Spring On A Buchan Ferm' Flora evokes the hope that comes with the ending of winter, "Noo, on a suddenty, the lift's rivven wide./ Hivvenly licht poors doon an blins and droons/ The dozent, thowless wardle. Snaa-bree loups,/ ice-tangles fae the eezins dreep, the Furth/ New quickent blinks an glinters i the sin." And yet spring itself holds its own dangers illustrated by the swift changes of the sky, "Syne, on the indraacht o a breath, the lift goams ower", and the lives and deaths of creatures living around the farm, "The lamming yowie yammers fae the bucht,/ The rottan's pykit teeth chudder the barley seck,/ The skweengin hoolet clooks the moosie's wyme,/ The ravenous futtrit sooks the livrock's breist." In many ways this poem epitomises the heart of Flora's poetry. We stand with her looking back upon the bleakness of the winter, hoping for a better future and yet around us the very real present hangs balanced and uncertain of its direction:

"Glory, an syne hertbrak, a sair oonchancy thing."

Taranis Books and Polygon publishers have a strong reputation for publishing new and innovative poetry. However *Case Histories & Other Poems* by Ellis Sopher published by Taranis and *Seeing the River* by Raymond Friel published by Polygon are poor collections.

Ellis Sopher's poems could have been written anywhere about anything. He could have been writing about a packet of Knorr Instant Soup for all the insight and depth these poems provide. What exactly does "Bandit Harry ... Red-eyed and dribbling" (from the poem 'Harry') tell us about the Gorbals or mental health care? Is Harry merely a name given to a space filled with Ellis' own preconceptions? The poems about Jewish culture are warmer yet even they lack any true insight. Certainly the poem Aunt Basalayeh tells us little Leah was "Small of stature, big of heart/ Your voice throaty with the juice/ Of freshly boiled gefilte fish" but what else? We learn Jewish words but that surely is not enough. The logic seems to be it is written therefore it is of interest.

Raymond Friel's saving grace is that his poetry is technically good. The poems about growing up, getting married, going on holiday... Events which could be interesting and even exciting – yet in Raymond's hands are terribly safe, indeed empty. Raymond's poetry is constrained and limited, completely void of any sense of adventure, daring, or wonder. In the poem 'A Talking To' his partner complains to him "You are so frightened/ Of anything/ That involves...risk!" And so he is. Reading this book is like being forced to look at badly taken holiday snaps or a wedding video - as indeed Raymond forces us to do in 'Billy and the Dolce Vita'. Raymond's own attempt at creating a point of reference is to mention his Irish background. However there is no insight of the Irish in Scotland – just the tedium of mass and burials and rosary beads. Yet Raymond need not remain such a stale poet. He has a certain skill but his writing is severely handicapped by his timidity and lack of imagination. He needs to abuse the canvas, throw paint everywhere, rip shreds off it, spit, kick, and reshape it with all the vigour he can muster.

Having finished reading Ellis and Raymond I couldn't help but feel that maybe it's time to call for a moratorium on Scottish male writers. And on first opening Jack Withers' *Balancing on a barbed wire fence* my moratorium musings were reinforced by an intro that referred to Jack as "the citizen poet". Personally I only know only one person who could lay claim to such a title (and he wouldn't): a front line dissident who had a breakdown after returning from Newbury, took up writing poetry to help recover – and as I write is in a cell underneath Glasgow Sheriff court for attempting to halt a nuclear convoy. And yet as I read Jack's book the more involved I became in his world. I found myself arguing, disagreeing, debating, agreeing, even laughing with the poet, and slowly but surely developing a very deep affection for his words and opinions.

"Let's halt a minute./ Only a minute? / It's so silent, so quiet./ Quite. Like being so close to a glimpse of the ultimate." And with these opening lines Jack Withers takes us on an astonishing journey through the universe seen from the perspective of a socialist in Scotland. Yeeee Ha! Jack treats language with that perfect mixture of contempt and respect that blasts his poems onwards and onwards yet always allows the reader to stay on board to enjoy the images and colours and ideas swirling about them. "The latest labour-leader,/ Phoney Stare/ sat contently in his/ don't-rock-the-boat rocking-chair/ clutching a big fat cat / or was it a teddy-bear? 'Phoney Stare'... Vast the distance now/ From our one-time home/ Star to quasar/ Our trajectory is not direct/ But circular/ On a great sweeping ring/ Curved/ Like a trembling cello-string/ Reverberating" 'No Return'... This is truly interactive poetry. If you need a break from the poem you're riding on, step off, visit another and come back again when you're ready. Jack tells us about Scotland, about love, about the working class, about humour and optimism and underneath it all – even at its blackest and angriest - the very beat and tempo of his poetry leaves the reader sharing a feeling of pride and dignity. I have no doubt the real citizen poet will also find it inspiring.

Rab Fulton

Strange flowers and electric butterflies

This Side of Reality: modern Czech writing, Alexandra Büchler (ed), Serpent's Tale, £8.99; *Nothing is Altogether Trivial: an anthology of writing from Edinburgh Review*, Murdo Macdonald (ed), EUP, £12.95; *Soho Square 7: New Scottish Writing*, Harry Ritchie (ed), Bloomsbury, £8.99.

Some poorer translations have Rimbaud's *"Que s'évadent d'étranges fleurs/ Et des papillons életriques"* as "Unfold strange flowers and electric butterflies". For the present work that this is a poor translation is irrelevant; what matters is that it was as this imperative I first came upon the lines, and it is following this imperative that all editors of anthologies (and indeed literary magazines) should be guided. This quotation is also apt as an anthology is, of course, a choice of flowers and there is no reason to bring attention to the common and familiar. I do not mean this in at all élitist manner. Rather an editor should bring us the rare and exotic from deepest Africa or the man-eating orchid from the Orient or the the latest pneumatic hybrids from the suburban laboratories and industrial estates of our own nation.

What flowers have these three editors brought back from the literary jungle? And are they electric? The answer to this second, in the case of Harry Ritchie's *Soho Square 7: New Scottish Writing* is most definitely not. Rather than venturing into the literary jungle that is Scotland, Mr. Ritchie's research could easily have amounted to scanning *Granta*'s Best of Young British Novelists and the current month's issue of *The Face*. Adventurous he is not, and the contents page which includes Candia McWilliam, William Boyd, Irvine Welsh, Robert Crawford, Alasdair Gray, Douglas Dunn, Tom Leonard etc sounds like a familiar litany which could be recited, mantra-style. Could it be possible that these authors are *not* known south of the border? From a publishing point of view this was a safe bet capitalising on a media generated trend.

Nevertheless, Ritchie's editorial conservatism cannot outweigh the sheer worth of the writing he include. Well written stories abound and particularly memorable is William Boyd's 'Loose Continuity' which shifts from pre-war Berlin to post-war Los Angeles featuring a young female architect. Echoes of *The Blue Afternoon*, I feel.

Even better though is John Burnside's 'Burning Elvis' which is one of the better stories I have read this year. A tale of suburban childhood – and here the ennui of suburbia transcends nation and could be anywhere West – it looks at the relationship between a precocious girl and the boy next door and the media as they photograph a burning effigy of Elvis Presley.

A L Kennedy takes her surgeon's knife to dissect another relationship. This time she looks at a British woman in America. One can only marvel at how well she draws her characters and captures the differences between the two cultures.

Also in this anthology is critical writing from Alasdair Gray on the Norman wasting of Old English and meditations on Scottish identity from Angus Calder, as well as poetry from Tom Leonard, Carol Ann Duffy, the now ubiquitous Robert Crawford and W N Herbert. It is however the short stories that stand out.

For an altogether better reader – for that is how it often seems – of contemporary Scottish literature, I should turn to Murdo Macdonald's *Nothing is Altogether Trivial: an anthology of writing from Edinburgh Review*. To some this might seem to be narcissistic vainglory from this onetime editor of that journal. In this respect Murdo Macdonald has more to prove than other the editors as here he surely is handling both his own work and that of other editors. A concession though: we often expect editors to be knowledgable of the field, even expert, and in this instance I doubt that none could be more so than Mr Macdonald. As to the charge of vainglory; the stories, poems, essays, interviews, and even reviews herein shirk that off with ease. Here gems lurk variously and darkly. This 'best of' contains a wealth of treasure too various to go into here. And why? Because *Nothing is Altogether Trivial* is a survey of Scottish culture or world culture in Scotland as it happened unlike *Soho Square 7* which is a survey of a Lahndan media-wave saying more about how Scotland is perceived rather than Scotland itself.

As a more recent issue of the *Edinburgh Review* told us, culture is a cosmorama, "a series of views of different parts of the world, tricked out with mirrors, lenses." The viewer (read here editor) of this is, must be an acquisitive, grabby magpie thing. But no matter how grabby the editor is, he can never show the whole, only the part, that part hopefully 'the best'. And this book's contents are as deep as they are wide. At this point I could do the unthinkable and quote the blurb. "This is a wide ranging, thought provoking, hugely enjoyable romp through the last ten years of Scottish writing." Alongside Kelman's bitter vernacular wit and Shenna Blackhall's brutally honest stories are rigorous essays. These range from the debate on New Glasgow painting, thoughts from authors on the writing (aonghas macneacail and W S Graham to the vigorous, dynamic, avant-garde (how could I possibly have missed it?!) *Neue Slowenische Kunst* (Charles Stephens). Here also is Alasdair Gray's now famous 'A Preface to an Anthology of Prefaces' and the invigorating power of George Davie's thought as he writes on Government and Nationalism in Scotland. This was written in 1969, and printed in the *Edinburgh Review* in 1990. It is still valid today, Davie's argument and language still as potent, still as strong. Davie asks us when we consider a devolved Scotland to bear in mind a Nationalist independent Scotland, and more importantly to remember and continue Scotland's theoretical academic tradition.

After all this my favourite piece was the title work, a review of two female American novelists by Jenny Turner printed in 1985. This is an as intelligent, as witty and as well written piece as one could hope to find. It combines two of my favourite characteristics – arrogance and subversiveness.

The strangest flowers though are to be found in Alexandra Büchler's *This Side of Reality: Modern Czech Writing* which follows writing from the immediate post-war period through to present-day, and begins with Ladislav Fuks evocative "Sadness is yellow and six pointed like a star of David. It was a great sadness." This sense of profound retrospective melancholy pervades the anthology. Many of the writers give a sense of terrible *ennui* waiting for something they know not what, while at the same time make the reader aware of the strange and fabulous – in that they are the stuff of fables – events taking place around them.

Perhaps one of the most useful stories in understanding the conditions of the Czech writer during the Cold War is Ivan Klíma's 'Tuesday Morning'. Here a former lover of the male narrator returns to Prague from where the narrator knows not. We are given an account of the old affair. She was married to whom she will not or cannot say and the affair consummated in a small glade outside the city during a summer. By winter though she managed to leave the country for the West. So on her return many years later after revisiting the glade, she poses the question why should an internationally renowned author not emigrate? The authorities would allow it.

Other stories and extracts reveal the feelings of a disoriented society uncertain of the boundaries of reality. The best examples are Michal Viewgh's extract from *The Blissful Years of Lousy Living* and Alexandra Berková from *The Sufferings of Devoted Lousehead*. But for a witty piece of magic realism showing hope thwarted turn to Michal Ajvas' 'The Beetle'. The author has been searching for details of a river and palace beneath Prague, in his search he has

> in vain read through forty-six volumes of the *Oxford Encyclopedia* which now burden my head shifting painfully inside my skull whenever I turn in bed at night – and now, all of a sudden, I find detailed instructions in a footnote on the page of a handbook on rabbit-breeding ... this footnote tells me that the door of the corridor leading to the malachite palace can be found in the back wall of an overstuffed wardrobe located in an apartment in the Prague district of Smíchov; it even gives the house number and the number of the apartment, but I cannot read the name of the street because of a beetle with shiny metallic wings who is sitting on precisely that spot, baring his enormous mandibles at me.

The beetle cannot be removed and for reasons of public hygiene all books are burnt on the same day as borrowing after which the library will be turned it to a market hall. "Just my luck as usual!"

From these seventeen authors, Büchler gives us a wide view of the writing of this people with an extraordinary literary tradition – it easy to forget that Prague was once a cultural centre to rival Vienna and Moscow while Berlin was a couple of market towns on the Spree. This is a fascinating and immensely enriching anthology.   *Samuel Wood*

Quiet Appreciation

Poetry Ireland Review, Issue 50, £5.99

This is the 50th issue in the third incarnation of *Poetry Ireland*. Under the editorial supervision of Michael Longley; poet and former Literary Director of the Northern Ireland Arts Council; it has an informed feel about it. Yet it is curiously static. There are no bad poems but, awkwardly for this reviewer who knows many of the contributors and considers himself a friend of long-standing with the editor, there are no new and exciting poems. Meticulous phrasing rather than stimulating ideas reign.

Apart from Tony Curtis's culling of Dennis O'Driscoll's regular compilation of quotes, *Pickings and Choosings*, the issue is entirely composed of verse. The individual poems are both invited by the editor from specific writers and selected by him from earlier issues. The well known are here: Heaney, Muldoon, Mahon, Hartnett and Kennelly. They are mixed with the comparatively unknown: Paula Meehan, Gerard Dawe, Eamonn Grennan and Rita Ann Higgings. there are some interesting new names: Katie Donovan, Kerry Hardie, Conor O Callaghan and, from Wales, Joyce Herbert. Yet even after several readings, there is a remarkable lack of celebration.

Poetry Ireland (first series: 1948-54) was founded by David Marcus in Cork. It published, among many, Samuel Beckett, C.D. Lewis and Brendan Behan. It had special issues featuring translations from the Gaelic and new American Verse.

The second series (1963-68), published by Liam Miller in his Dublin based Dolmen Press, was edited by John Jordan (1930-1988). These were exciting times. Literary movements, away from the influences of Yeats and Joyce, were reflected in the small A2 paperbacked format. The fastidious editor sought and got the best from his contributors. These included original work from Thomas Kinsella, Pearse Hutchinson, Austin Clarke, Seamus Heaney, Michael Hartnett, Eavan Boland, Eithne Strong and indeed Longley himself.

The journal was revived in its present form as *Poetry Ireland Review* by John F. Deane in 1981. In 1991, under the management of Theo

Dorgan, it became "the organ of Eigse Eireann/Poetry Ireland", an organisation set up by Deane and now central to a number of literary activities across the borders of island Ireland.

It adapted an admirable policy of retaining different editors for set periods. This had led to a stimulating shift of emphasis. Number 31 (Spring 1991), with editorial guidance from Maire Mhac an Saoi, had a 100 page Scottish supplement collated by William Neill. In 1992 Peter Denham initiated a series of regular items and interviews which added depth and background to contemporary Irish publishing and literary mores. In 1994, with its youngest yet editor, the poet and fiction writer Pat Boran (b. 1963), it had an issue (No. 41) devoted to *Sexuality*. "A subject that too often seems ignored, or sanitized, in the publishing world", said the editiorial. "Ah well, youth", as Leopold Bloom said in *Ulysses* (1922), "has no time for remembering pleasure".

In its time *Poetry Ireland* has moved from the basement in Herbert Place, a library in Upper Mount Street, to its present attic closet in the one-time seat of British colonialism Dublin castle overlooking Viking remains, Norman cathedrals, Georgian tenements and the River Liffey. Its patrons have moved from being Monument Creameries (John Ryan) to Grogans Bar in South William Street (Tommy Smith). Its readership embraces the Americas and prison libraries in Britain. It publishes, on average, over twenty new writers a year. It is now, more or less, a regular quarterly. The annual subscription is £20.00 (Bermingham Tower, Upper Yard, Dublin Castle, Dublin 2, Ireland).

Unfortunately Michael Longley fails to record any of this information or background in his editorial. A pity. One-off editors should use such occasions to record the achievements of the past for the present and the future. Maybe this is the warped perspective of an exile. For the successes in the past are reflected in the confidence in new work from writers as different as Paul Muldoon and Thomas McCarthy. The brilliantly selected "rediscovered poems" include Eavan Boland's marvellous *At the Glass Factory in Cavan Town* and Peter Sirr's gently evolving emotional macaronic *Oasis* wherein "the light itself (is) seeming to deepen".

The complete result, however, is disappointing. It was a salutary guide to the source of my unease to reread Thomas Kinsella's stern stricture on contemporary literary levels in Ireland. "It's not one of the lucky times. There's a lot of bad poetry, bad poets, bad critics and bad readers."

This seemed unfortunately close to the familiar that haunts and guides me. This reviewer has, at times, been guilty on all accounts. But there was another itch irritating the critic-conscience. It was the absences. I missed among the contributors Kinsella himself, John F. Deane, Seamus Deane, Paul Durcan, Eilean Ni Chuilleanain, Pearse Hutchinson, Hugh Maxton and myself. With gathering unease I realised my criticism was based on reflective discontent.

But then looking back on the omission I suddenly realised that the figure most missed in the pages was Longley himself. By now I have almost convinced myself that he too is avoiding the applause of the clique to allow other readers appreciate the quiet.

Hayden Murphy

Who do we think we are?

Grant, Alexander/Stringer, Keith J (eds.), *Uniting the Kingdom: The Making of British History*. Routledge Pittock, Murray G H, *The Myth of the Jacobite Clans*, Edinburgh University Press, Szechi, Daniel (ed.), *'Scotland's Ruine' Lockhart of Carnwath's Memoirs of the Union* Association for Scottish Literary Studies

This clutch of books is a tribute to the liveliness of the debates which we are currently raging in the academic and political life of the United Kingdom over the issue of national identity. As soon as the phrase 'national identity' is used in the singular in the UK, confusion and ambiguity is guaranteed. Though the UK may be an over-centralized political system, the 'national' adjective usually associated with it, which is 'British', is itself ambiguous to the point where it appears to confuse even those, who like Dr. Nick Tate, a chief executive of the Governments's School Curriculum and Assessment Authority, are paid to define it. In *Uniting the Kingdom*, he is cited as saying that 'majority culture' must be inculcated in schools by stress on "English language, English history and literary heritage, and the study of Christianity and the classical world". The implicit cultural arrogance of the English-dominated Westminster political ascendancy, of which Dr Tate and his like are mere tools, could hardly be better demonstrated. Equally insidious is the frequently violent hostility of the 'terrible simplifiers' to the fact that complex multiple identities are a normal, healthy reality among the inhabitants of the UK.

Uniting the Kingdom had its origins in an Anglo-American Conference of Historians held in the summer of 1994 at the Institute of Historical Research in London. Invaluable though the resulting volume is, events have moved fast enough to date some of its assumptions. The introduction, for example, contains the mandatory contemporary favourable reference to the Northern Ireland 'Peace Process', seen as setting the problems of the province well on the way to 'solution'. In retrospect the process was as inherently flawed as the other American-hyped 'peace-process' in the Middle East, and for broadly similar reasons. Never did the IRA contemplate anything except unconditional surrender to its definition of what 'Irishness' is, and what it is not allowed to be, if necessary under penalty of death.

So the historical roots of problems and attitudes which plague, harass, and threaten us, do matter. It is only by facing them honestly that we can move the debate to levels of reality which may discredit those who wish to impose their definitions of allowable identities on us, from the elected dictator at Westminster to the cultural imperialist behind the assassin's gun. For the purposes of wide-ranging analysis over time and the whole archipelago, *Uniting the Kingdom* is the most important of these three books, and David Cannadine's excellent contribution on British History as a 'new subject' brilliantly stresses the fact that though 'four nation' history would be a vast improvement on the extreme anglocentricity which has for long been the unchallenged orthodoxy, it is not the only defensible approach. The Highlands-Lowlands dichotomy crosses national borders, as does the Gaeltacht. Provinces around the Dalriadic sea like Argyll, Ulster, Ayrshire and Galloway may be expected to have much in common.

What emerges from the second section of this book is how deeply modern problems are rooted in medieval precedents. James Campbell shows how early the West Saxon monarchy established England as a unitary kingdom, uniformly administered through enduring institutions such as the shires. Subsequent contributions stress both the way the Anglo-Normans seized this heritage and drove it outwards as they sought to subject the archipelago, and their late-medieval loss of dynamism. England was left with Irish provinces; disgruntled Celtic 'barbarians' on and inside its expanded frontiers; and a hate-love relationship with suspicious Scots.

The third section of the book, devoted to early-modern period, centres on the era between 1603 and 1707 when the accession of the Stuarts to the English and Irish thrones created a multiple-kingdom based monarchy. Given the scale of devolution this implied, Conrad Russell is surely right to say that the prime responsibility for the terrible mess into which relations between the kingdoms had fallen by 1641, leading to the War of the Three Kingdoms, must rest with King Charles I.

98

Nick Canny shrewdly adds a large measure of responsibility for the crisis to the account of James I whose failure to meet and fight the Counter-Reformation in Ireland in its early vulnerable phase, allowed an unbridgeable chasm to open within that kingdom and between it and the others.

The modern section sees Peter Marshall stress that if empire became an important part of British identity, especially after 1792, the adamant refusal of the Westminster political system to accept any form of power-sharing meant there could not be an indefinite global future for Britishness. The readiness of the Conservative party to ditch Ireland, and its Unionist communities, in 1922, is, as John Turner's piece demonstrates, fresh evidence that Westminster seeks above all its own survival, unchanged. David Marquand argues that the 'market imperialism' of the Thatcher era, when big money set out to buy control of politics, justice, and social relations, necessarily strained the coherence of the UK, and John Pocock closes the book with a characteristically subtle reminder of the fact that sustained ambiguity and debate may itself be an element in modern British identity.

So where does all this leave Scotland? Murray Pittock's book is primarily a contribution to Jacobite studies, but it is also by definition a contribution to the ongoing literary argument about the extent to which Scots, and more particularly Lowland Scots, had by 1745 acquiesced in the new British identity which had been foisted on them by the Act of Union of 1707. An excellent historiographical introduction makes the point that a whole succession of historians from J R Green, to Sir Winston Churchill, and including such modern professional luminaries as Roy Campbell, Paul Langford and Linda Colley, have deprecated the significance of the last Jacobite rising by stating that it had no serious Lowland support, and was little more than a surprise coup by a few thousand 'backward' Highlanders. In his next chapter 'Children of the Mist', Pittock himself a literary scholar and expert on Jacobite verse, admits that one contributory factor to the strength of the exclusively Highland myth of Jacobitism was the use by contemporary Jacobite propagandists of the figure of the Highlander as the ideal Scottish patriot. Pittock's own answer to the myth is not new. I said much the same in four books on Jacobitism published in the 1980's (the last one co-authored with John S Gibson). However, the myth of the 'primitive' and exclusively Highland nature of Jacobitism is so tenacious that the counter-argument cannot be repeated too often and Pittock's book is based on two interesting contentions. The first is original and wholly convincing: that the military effort put forth by the Scottish Jacobites compares very well with the much-vaunted effort mounted by the seventeenth-century Covenanting regime in Scotland. The second contention is pushed beyond the defensible when Pittock re-interprets figures in an unpublished thesis to exaggerate the Lowland element in the Jacobite forces in 1745-46 (mainly by treating far too much of Perthshire as 'Lowland'). It does not really subvert his main point: there was a large Lowland element in the Jacobite rising, even if its shock troops were Highland.

Daniel Szechi's excellent new edition of Lockhart of Cornwath's memoirs of the making of the 1707 Union and of the abortive Franco-Jacobite invasion of 1708 is to be welcomed. It is the first since the pirated 1714 edition, and the authorised 1817 edition, on which Szechi's is based. To Szechi's biographical and historical notes, Paul Scott adds notes on textual variations. Lockhart is partisan, but historically remarkably reliable. His resounding denunciation of Daniel Defoe's shameless attempt to deny the massive reality of widespread Scottish disaffection towards the Act of Union buttresses Pittock's key first chapter. The Act of Union always was contentious; is now contentious; and deserves to be contentious.

Bruce P Lenman

A History i' the Scots

William Wallace – A Scots Life, Glenn Telfer, Argyll Publishing, £6.99; *Robert The Bruce – A Scots Life*, Glenn Telfer, Argyll Publishing, £6.99;

These attractively produced paperbacks are the first to appear in a planned series of biographies of famous Scots, both men and women, aimed at young readers from 13 upwards. Such biographies have appeared before, but the difference is that these books in the *Scots Legend* series are written in Scots. In the case of Wallace and Bruce it is claimed that they represent the first new work in Scots on our national heroes since the original mediaeval epics of Blind Harry and John Barbour.

The language used is not the Scots of Burns or MacDiarmid, to be sure, but a simple and lively idiom that may be heard every day in the playground or on the bus – as the author has said, "about halfway between Oor Wullie and Lorimer".

Glenn Telfer has avoided vesting Wallace and Bruce with mystic or superhuman powers. He has instead attempted to give a historically accurate and realistic account of the known facts, mingled with imagination and psychological insight, building up a credible picture of these two heroes with their faults as well as their qualities. At the same time he emphasises the spirit of courage, loyalty and unshakeable desire for independence which drove them. He also manages to give a coolly objective account of the character and motivation of Edward I. His descriptions of the various battles are gorily vivid, and he has not neglected to point out the terrible effects on ordinary people, both Scots and English, of the years of warfare.

But the talking point of this series will inevitably be the use of the Scots language. It is not so long ago that the use of a good Scots word in school might be frowned on, or worse, but a revolution has taken place in our classrooms both in the use of Scots and also in the teaching of our own history; teachers as well as general readers may find this series very welcome.

The books are easy to read and have a short glossary of words which might not be so familiar. My worry is that too many ponderous English words and phrases pepper the text, holding up the narrative and undermining its purpose. Little attempt has been made to use Scots equivalents for abstract terms. This is not always possible, but one does not have to dredge a dictionary to find, for example, such words as 'daithless' or 'bumbazed' which have a more satisfying ring than 'immortal' or 'confused'.

There is also some inconsistency in the Scots spelling which one hopes will be ironed out in future books. (No space here to enter into controversy about Standard Scots!) Errors have also crept into some of the English words, such as "it's" for "its". But these are teething troubles. These books are a breakthrough.

It is a sign of the great changes in the linguistic and political scene in Scotland, and a tribute to all those writers, teachers and others who have laboured to bring about this change, that Argyll Publishing has had the confidence to produce this series. I wish it well.

Heather Scott

Pamphleteer

The past two years have seen the revival of many a Scottish hero: William Wallace's fight against the English, Rob Roy's uprising, the adventures of drug-addicted, trainspotting 'local heroes'. Yet above all, alive and kicking, singing his way into the Scottish psyche, and certainly not a dead poet, is the unforgettable Robert Burns. Scotland dedicated last year to this remarkable local bard. And who else could commemorate the bicentenary of Robert Burns better than a true people's poet? *Robert Burns – A Poem* by Iain Crichton Smith (Morning Star Publications, £2) is a respectful, 15 stanza poem, full with characteristically vivid imagery, formal elegance and highly professional, deceptive simplicity: "Robert Burns, how much has been said about you as if you were a Bible to which we always return..." Once again, the myth of the rustic plough-man is celebrated, this story about women and love, wine and poverty, pain and genius recalled. It's "a journey towards perpetual debts and an early death", Crichton Smith declares, drawing the (now only too familiar) picture of a simple heroic Scotsman outsmarting an oppressive upper-class. The flowing rhythmic movements of the poem draw the reader into a bygone world, setting an admirably 'quiet' monument to a recently and loudly admired artist. The last line of the work leaves us with as much as nothing – Burn's "zigzag skeleton" – a myth, unpredictable, ungraspable.

Round about Burns, a publication by The Stewarty Museum in Kirkcudbright (£2) constitutes an interesting contribution to last year's 'Burns hype'. It, too, marks the poet's bicentenary, yet it aims to demonstrate that Burns did not write in a literary vacuum. The anthology presents a collection of poetry written in and around Dumfries and Galloway from Burn's time up to the early 20th century. The 28 annotated works of these 18 largely forgotten or unrecognised authors have been grouped under the themes of Labour and Politics, Love, Nature and the Supernatural, and Time and Life. Their tone is playful, the atmosphere of rustic naivety, sprinkled with humour and human emotions. They provide a rounded literary, political and historical background to Burns himself, his time and region. John Hudson, the editor of the selection, surely did a praiseworthy job in bringing to attention the range and quantity of poetry published in Burns' home county.

Jumping forward into the noise and turmoil of twentieth century Scotland, socially and politically minded poetry lovers should have a close look at Rab Fulton's *lyrical poems* (Hybrid, £3). His dynamic, energetic use of modern Scots is certainly an experience not to be missed. The language is at times stressful and bare, loaded with conflict and emotions. Already the cover photograph of demonstrators and policemen suggests what the reader can expect and the publisher promises: "...a sweeping, breathtaking journey through the year 1995 and the political climate in the Strathclyde region." Among the topics are arrests and police raids, actions against environmentalists and the political Left, unemployment. I only wished that Hybrid had delivered accompanying translations in order to enable more non-Scots speaking readers to enjoy this exciting modern voice.

Highcliff Press has recently published two new editions of fine Scottish poetry – *For everything must be returned* by Andrew Fox and *Lady on a stained Glass Fire-Escape* by Pete Faulkner (both available at £2.50). Although I could not bring myself to share much enthusiasm for the first (despite the original title), I genuinely enjoyed reading Faulkner's almost rhymeless verse. Vivid imagery and an incredible evocation of mood characterise his style. Here we encounter poetry that is alive and breathing. He leads us skilfully to Gringos in Mexico, a fiddler on a porch in the southern States, only to abandon us with a girl on a park bench and a man rising from sleep, somewhere, anywhere. His often isolated sentences remind one of flickering video clips, still-lives of a moment:

Young trees grow through an abandoned car
Browned Photographs fade on a vanished wall
Young boys by the roadside hold up dead iguanas
We cannot tell the starfish from the stars

It is a staccato of haunting images and shattered pieces of information that are able to form a new poem about the age-old topic of human alienation and loneliness. Not very original, you might say, yet masterly handled.

Moving down to England, Robert Roberts *Third selection of Poems* (Pikestaff, £2) is as quiet as the subtitle 'Reflections from the Otter Valley' indicates. This is poetry by a talented craftsman to be appreciated and enjoyed. Roberts seems to distance himself from the turbulence and instability of contemporary urban life in order to retreat into a calmer rural atmosphere. Everywhere in his work are signs of the struggle between man and nature. At times, mythology and ancestral influence break through. I liked 'Hylas', in which modern television rituals and the presentation of news are crisply equalised with "the job of those old myths" – both there to install fear and awe and a bit of sensationalism in the audience; there to provide us with a brief glimpse of absolute feelings.

From the publishing house Acumen comes *Mushroom Lane* by Christopher J P Smith (£2.25). This is another charming work, steeped in ancient Greek and Roman mythology. Smith's handling of verse is witty, spiced with a wry sense of humour, as the end of 'A Letter from Ovid' demonstrates: "Wine is finished. I cannot eat this mess. I'm off to take our story to the press." His directness is refreshing! The title of the collection refers to a long poem placed at the end of the pamphlet, which I however did not enjoy as much as the rest of his writing. In 'Cymru Nouveaux' Smith writes: "I'm sick of hearing the new Celts up from Oxford or Jutland with their talk of torques and poets who are really politicians". Six stanzas later he ends with the words: "But I love the green rivers and watervoices free of taints, industry and druids. You can sometimes fish there in absolute peace." These lines capture the main voice of his poems: nature-bound, with a strong dislike of too much talk and false traditionalism.

Cornish Links by the Kenow Poets Press (£4.95) is an anthology of contemporary Cornish poetry written in English. I recommend it to all those who are interested in the regional poetry of Cornwall. The works contain precise articulations of landscape and are full of local colour and mood. With merry laughter, they compel the reader to dwell in its inviting scenery.

A number of new publications have been brought out by the Canadian publisher Mekler & Deahl. The works are mainly by Ontario writers and display a large range of artistry from across the big water. Among them are three anthologies, *A Cliff Runs Through* (£5), *Ingots* (£5) and *Mix Six* (£6), offering a selection of verse by some of Canada's finest poets still to be discovered in Europe. *Not to Rest in Silence*, available for £3, constitutes a celebration of Canada's People's Poetry, a movement from the late 50s which drew inspiration from Carl Sandburg. As editor Terry Barker explains in the foreword, its intention is to recover dimensions of common human experience in all its facets, obscured by the artificiality of bourgeois existence.

I relished Glasgow-born Simon Frank's *imaginary poems* (£5), divided into three groups: imaginary, silly and simple. One of the first poems in this collection rushes us violently to the core of the author's concern with poetry and expression: "When he smashed his head open on the concrete he was an artist whose colours came straight from the heart". At times he experiments with letters, sizes and graphic styles of writing and makes extensive use of repetitions. Poetry is thoughts written down, Frank states on the very first page, and that image could sum up his attempt to free poetry from the vault in which it has often been locked. While reading, I could not help thinking that the simplicity of his verse might have something in stock for everybody, but especially for younger readers.

Very different in tone and style is Albert WJ Harper's booklet *Poems of Reflections* (£6). It is an appeal to the harmony of sound and sense, a powerful rhythmic compulsion, that will be appreciated, as Harper hopes, by all those who acknowledge dignity as an ideal in human affairs and nature.

It is well worth spending time with these new national and international publications, well worth paying some tribute to the sometimes underestimated art of – to speak in Simon Frank's terms – 'writing down thoughts'.

Eva Freischläger

Catalogue

This column is intended to mention books, mainly of merit, which we are unable to review. I can think of few books more fitting this category than *Cry Bosnia* by Paul Harris, (Canongate, £14.95). Harris has done much to alert us to the plight of Bosnia, and the appalling atrocities both ancient and newly invented which have characterised 'the Balkan War', as a result of being prepared himself to get into the thick of things. This handsome book, amply illustrated with both black and colour photographs is the result, and proceeds go towards the Bosnia welfare effort. Introduced by Paddy Ashdown, the backbone of the book is a long essay by Harris, stemming often from very personal reminiscences, his experience and knowledge of the war. We aren't spared the horrors – why should we be – but it nonetheless keeps a hold on humanity and optimism. This book you should have, for many reasons, not least quality, and we should leave it ears ringing with Harris's last words: "It is the struggle of the whole of Europe for peace, democracy, cultural diversity and tolerance against the evil forces of Fascism. That is why we must make a stand."

One of the most heroic projects now in train is Carcanet's step-by-step publication of the bulk of Hugh MacDiarmid's *oeuvre*. It is a gargantuan task, manfully steered by editor, Alan Riach, a Scottish poet teaching at New Zealand's University of Waikato. One landmark in MacDiarmid's literary career was his essays in *Contemporary Scottish Studies* between 1925 and 27, setting out the parameters for a new vision of Scottish cultural identity. These are now available (£25.00 hardback), cheap considering the riches it contains. The themes are literature, language, literary and cultural criticism, music and historiography, education and it includes essays on the likes of Charles Murray, Violet Jacob, Neil M Gunn, the Burns Cult and many other persons and subjects. This book is key to understanding 20th century Scottish culture and, in its text and presentation, a tremendous academic achievement.

Sue Innes has been a pioneer in women's studies in Scotland. Her knowledge and wisdom on this subject accumulated over more than 20 years are channelled into *Making it*

Work, Women, Change and Challenge (Chatto & Windus, £12.99). Her central question, prompted by the 1993 75th anniversary of women's suffrage, is what has changed for women in Britain, and what has not. This is a pertinent question, for growing affluence has provoked complaisance about the true state of women. Brooking no nonsense, Innes tackles the main aspects of women's lives: love, family, social problems, to Scotland's changing political awareness and the women's role in it. After thorough exposition, she reaches what seems an unarguable conclusion, that women's 'issues' are not mere middle class concern, but part of "a serious and visionary attempt to address inequality" which would "power the renewal of our society which is so badly needed." This perspicacious book should be compulsory reading for both sexes.

I sometimes feel tempted to run a competition for the whackiest idea for an anthology.) One recently published anthology we should be pleased to have, is *Working Words: Scottish Creative Writing*, edited by Valerie Thornton (Hodder & Stoughton, £5.99). At that it's a snip, as well as being a good idea. It combines useful tips for those who wish, or for educational reasons must, pursue creative writing with well-chosen texts drawn from current Scottish literature, so the models are directly relevant to the experience of those who might wish to emulate them – gratifyingly different from all those 'How To . . .' books. Thornton selects widely from current practitioners, from Iain Crichton Smith and Janice Galloway to Gordon Meade and Helen Lamb, two fine but less well known writers. *Shouting it Out*, edited by Tom Pow (Hodder & Stoughton), has the simpler agenda of being an anthology of stories from contemporary Scotland, but he has chosen well, including Janet Paisley and Bess Ross alongside Brian McCabe and A L Kennedy, and usefully provides an autobiographical statement from each author.

Ian MacDougall has done much digging in Scottish history. From Mercat Press (£13.99) comes his *Voices From War*, recollections of war by Scottish men and women. Included are testimonials from Harry McShane, Scots poet J K Annand, Dorothy Wiltshire and conscientious objector Norman MacCaig, who ends with the brusque assertion: "I just refused to kill people." Many other points of view and experiences of course are expressed in this valuable book, which alas due to the small print is a struggle to read. From the same stable comes *The Ghost o' Mause and other Tales and Traditions of East Perthshire* by Maurice Fleming. These are also user-unfriendly – pity, because they are readable, intriguing pieces drawn from authentic sources.

There is an increasing interest in Scottish social culture and topography. Birlinn have published much in this field, recently two very consultable two volumes, *Scottish Proverbs* compiled by Colin S K Walker and *Scottish Customs*, by Sheila Livingstone, both £5.99. On the outdoor front, also Birlinn, are *Highways and Byways in the West Highlands* and *the Central Highlands* (£9.99). Both volumes are full of the lore, history and culture as well as the landscape of these areas, divertingly written (apart again for the small print – I wouldn't take them out on a walk if I were you).

Gradually more books appear on drama (not an area adequately treated by the publishing industry. John Donald deserve a special pat on the back for Priscilla Barlow's biography of Duncan MacRae, *Wise Enough to Play the Fool* (£14.95) which provides a rounded, insightful portrait of that great Scottish actor (foreword by Stanley Baxter). New writing from the Royal Court Theatre is supplied in Faber & Faber's *Coming on Strong* (£9.99). I wish more theatres would also publish the new plays they produce. Phil Jones's *Drama as Therapy, Theatre as Living* (Routledge) is more intended for the professional, but contains insights also for those interested in psychology and the arts generally. From Routledge also is the slightly daunting *Contemporary Plays by Women of Colour*, edited by Kathy A Perkins and Roberta Uno, including plays by Terry Gomez and Elizabeth Wong, and I commend it for the social range and raunchy anarchy of the work. Runetree (PO Box 1035, London, W2 6ZX) have shown remarkable initiative and courage in publishing radio plays by Scottish writer, Menzies McKillop, known to *Chapman* readers. They have issued the pamphlet *The Battle of Maldon* (£2.50) and the slim volume, three plays, *Cuthbert, Columba* and *Caedmon* (£5.75). Although all are historical in content, the dia-

logue is racy and dramatic. Perhaps here I can mention Edinburgh Royal Lyceum's useful study pack for *The Steamie* and the National Theatre for Scotland Campaign's persuasive propaganda pamphlet: *The Scottish Stage Reaches the Page*, (The Netherbow, £2.00). We could do with more of this kind of thing.

Another neglected area is Scottish traditional song, and here The Hardie Press, working with Traditional Song and Music and Song Association (TMSA) have shown both wisdom and enterprise in commissioning and publishing *Come Gie's a Sang*, 73 songs edited by Sheila Douglas. The book, music and words, is clearly set out, and you can find there authentic versions of favourites 'Macpherson's Rant' and 'Bonny Ythanside' to many lesser-known songs you'll be thoroughly glad to make the acquaintance of. This is the kind of book you won't want to lend to your friends.

Returning briefly to Scottish landscape, Alastair Scott's *Native Stranger: a Journey in Familiar and Foreign Scotland* (Little, Brown and Co, £16.99) is a delightful voyage of discovery from Out Skerries in Shetland to the Mull of Galloway, celebrating the land and the culture, and dropping in, for tea as it were, on Sorley MacLean and George Mackay Brown, summoning up the wraiths of Robert Burns and Mary Queen of Scots, and, of course, not forgetting the ubiquitous midges. For those religiously inclined, Floris Books have provided the handsome *Illustrated Life of Columba* (£12.99) and *Sea-Road of the Saints* (£9.99) both by John Marsden. The latter scans the Scottish Western coastline in search of Celtic holy men. Religion and landscape also figure large in a new novel by Ann Lingard, another *Chapman* writer, (Headline Review, £16.99), a simply but powerful story of a woman living on a remote Scottish island searching for spiritual and personal healing.

The Clarendon Press (Oxford) show a continuing commitment to Scotland with the detailed and instructive volume by R D Anderson, *Education and the Scottish People, 1750-1913*, outrageously priced at £40, whereas Polygon maintain a more egalitarian approach with Andrew Lockhart Walker's lively, challenging development of the ideas of George Elder Davie, *The Revival of the Democratic Intellect*, a snip at £13.95.   *Joy Hendry*

Notes on Contributors

Pamela Beasant comes from Glasgow and has been living in Orkney for ten years. A short collection, *On Orkney*, was published by Galdragon Press in 1991.

Margaret Elphinstone is the author of three novels: *The Incomer, A Sparrow's Flight* and *Islanders* and a book of short stories. She has two daughters and lives in Ayrshire.

Una Leonie Flett, born in India, educated in Scotland. First career in professional ballet. Author of *Revisting Empty Houses, Falling from Grace* and many short stories. Now lives in Southern Spain.

Eva Freischläger is a Comparative Literature graduate currently volunteering at Chapmans and teaching German in Glasgow.

Rab Fulton is a Scottish socialist republican, poetry widely published in countless magazines and is actively involved in pro-democracy campaigns.

Nigel Grant is Emeritus Professor of Education at the University of Glasgow. He has published books and many articles on Scottish and international themes.

George Gunn's most recent book *Whins* was published by Chapman 1996. He has recently performed some of his poems on Radio Scotland's documentary "Coastlands".

Brent Hodgson: submits poetry and fiction to literary outlets regularly as the sight of a postman with an empty sack makes him go doo-lally.

Bruce Lenman is Professor of Modern History at St. Andrews University. He has written books on Scottish economic and social history, Jacobitism, and colonial wars.

Maurice Lindsay: once programmer for Border Television. His many publications include *The Burns Encyclopaedia* and *The History of Scottish Literature*.

Ann MacKinnon is a teacher in Dumbarton. She has had poetry published in *West Coast* and *Understanding* magazines.

Alan MacGillivary lectures in Scottish Literature and has recently edited a book on the teaching of Scottish Literature.

Pàdraig Maclabhruinn was born in 1950, and works as a teacher and translator in Edinburgh. He is married with two children.

Neil McNeil: widely published poet, lives in Sauchie, tutors creative writing workshops, does reading. More than happy to be published again after four years of silence.

Gordon Meade: former writer-in-residence for Dundee. His second collection *The Scrimshaw Sailor* (1996) published by Chapman. Lives in Fife with his family.

James Miller lives near Inverness and has been writing for years. His latest book is *A Wild and Open Sea*. Poetry in his native Caithness dialect is a recent venture.

Hayden Murphy born Dublin 1945. Poet and Arts journalist. Latest publication Exile's Journal (Galdragon Press: 1992).

Stuart A. Paterson: an Ayrshireman, born 1966. *Saving Graces*, a poetry collection, published early '97 (diehard). Likes good folk music, Scorsese movies, Roerich's paintings. .

David Punter has been published in various magazines; his most recent collection of poems is *Asleep at the Wheel* (1996). He is the worst squash player in Scotland.

Heather Reyes currently lives in Essex. She divides her time between teaching and research at London University.

Derek Ross: was born in Stranraer in 1956, now lives in Dumfries. He spends his spare time writing, taking photographs and defending his town of origin.

Hugh Clark Small was born in Lanarkshire, lives in Edinburgh. His collection, *Cusp*, was published by Cru Publishing.

Heather Scott born London 1935. Married poet Tom Scott 1963. Has occasionally contributed poetry and prose to magazines.

Gerry Stewart is an adopted Scot and is busy trying to find time to write letters and poetry.

Pippa Stuart: married name Orr, one husband, one son, keen Francophile and votes Liberal.

Gael Turnbull's most recent book of poems is *For Whose Delight* from Mariscat Press.

Cathy Wright is 30 and an English graduate from Strathclyde University. She writes articles, short stores and (someday, when she gets time!) novels.